CURIOSITIES OF
CENTRAL NEW YORK

MELANIE ZIMMER

Charleston   London

THE
History
PRESS

Published by The History Press
Charleston, SC 29403
www.historypress.net

Copyright © 2012 by Melanie Zimmer
All rights reserved

<Cover Image Info>

First published 2012

Manufactured in the United States

ISBN 978.1.60949.666.1

Library of Congress CIP data applied for.

This book is dedicated to all the magical and legendary creatures of Central New York.

CONTENTS

CONTENTS

ACKNOWLEDGEMENTS

I will attempt to thank the many marvelous people and institutions who have assisted me in the research for this book or have granted permission to use images. Many thanks to:

The Cazenovia Public Library for granting permission to use photographs of Hen and other related displays and the transcription of "The Mummy Tea Party."

The Lorenzo State Historic Site, operated by the New York State Parks' Office of Recreation and Historic Preservation, for allowing me to view Robert James Hubbard's diary.

The Georgetown Historical Society for images of the Muller Château, as well as information on The Spirit House.

Edith Monsour for information on the Jenkins house, family and horses and for allowing me to visit and photograph the secret room in the false cistern in her basement.

Aaron S. Popple for his story on the Little People of Whitelaw.

Madis Senner for the information he has shared on the Spirit House.

Josyln Godwin for sending me a copy of his book *The Spirit House, or Brown's Free Hall in Georgetown, NY: A Short History*, which contained marvelous information and historical articles in the appendix that were both interesting and useful in telling that legendary tale.

Matthew Urtz, the historian for Madison County, New York. He and his team searched endless historical files of old county court cases looking for information I wanted but to no avail. Though the information is not contained in this book, those folks still deserve a heartfelt thanks for their Herculean effort.

ACKNOWLEDGEMENTS

Historian Mary Messere, otherwise known as "Back Street Mary," for directing me to helpful people in my searches.

Gail Putnam, curator of the Remsen-Steuben Historical Society collection, who helped me find the information I needed on Dr. Roberts of Steuben.

Beverly Choltco-Devlin, reference and electronic resources consultant at the Mid York Library System, for her help locating reference material regarding Iroquois witchcraft.

Susan Jones, park ranger at Fort Stanwix National Monument, for her Oneida Indian version of the Giant Mosquito tale.

Whitney Tarella, commissioning editor at The History Press, for asking me to write this book.

And finally, my husband, Francis, who has slowly watched me become swallowed by a great sea of papers in my study and has never mentioned my disappearance to anyone.

INTRODUCTION
THERE WAS,
THERE WAS NOT...

When I was a girl, I desperately wished that fairies were real. One day, I headed out to the side of our house to a part of the yard that was not used much and heavily shaded by several large juniper bushes, and I built a small home for the fairies using whatever natural materials were available, dirt, bark, leaves and such. I then left it, hoping that the fairies would find it to their liking and occupy it. I checked back periodically over the weeks and months, but as far as I could ascertain, there was never anybody living there save a few stray pill bugs. I watched and waited until, at last, the fairy home fell into disrepair, still devoid of occupants, much to my disappointment. Now, past my fiftieth birthday, I have yet to see a fairy, but I still cannot say they don't exist. In fact, as you will read, an acquaintance of mine has been more fortunate than I have been in respect to fairy sightings.

I would like to invite the reader to join me on a mysterious journey into the myths, legends and curiosities of Central New York. We won't be traveling far, and you don't have to pack a bag, but you will likely be amazed at the wonders that exist so close to home. Not everyone realizes that Central New York has a remarkable, legendary past that includes tales of witchcraft, giants, Little People, lake monsters and giant mosquitoes as well as flying heads. Along the way, you will meet a two-thousand-year-old mummy, visit a house designed by spirits and ponder the mystery of a village built on a hill by a mysterious man operating under the alias of "Louis Muller." But all this is just a taste of what you will find here in Central New York. So join me on this small journey of discovery. You may just be surprised at what you'll find.

Fairy tales often begin with "Once upon a time." However, not all fairy tales begin in that way. In some traditions, they begin with "There was, there was not," and I think that captures the essence of these stories. Let's begin our journey now, with a deep breath, a simple turn of the page and a step into the world of imagination.

There was, there was not...

CHAPTER ONE
WITCHCRAFT

O ne would expect to find numerous early cases of settlers in Central New York practicing witchcraft. Certainly, other states were trying witches in court, clear evidence that some believed in witchcraft, if not its actual practice; yet unlike other areas in America at this time, no records of witchcraft trials in the early days of this region exist. Still, here in Central New York, there is one remarkable story of the legendary Dr. Daniel Roberts, denizen of Steuben, known to locals as "the witch doctor." Also at this time, members of the six Iroquois Nations practiced "witchcraft," and those who were caught were punished for participating in such activity.

THE STORY OF DR. DANIEL ROBERTS, THE WITCH DOCTOR OF STEUBEN

Years ago in Steuben, not far from the burial site of Baron von Steuben, stood a home known to area residents as "the witch doctor's house." The house is now long gone, but stories of the witch doctor, Doctor Daniel Roberts, still remain. Like many men in the Steuben and Remsen area, Dr. Roberts was a Welshman. But he was no ordinary Welshman.

Daniel Roberts was born in 1775 near Land's End in Wales and was reared in the parish of Llaniestyn nearby. As a young man, he attended the local chapel where he one day listened to an itinerant preacher. Daniel was so inspired that he felt a calling within, a calling that he understood to be from God, and Daniel decided he wanted to become a preacher. Although ıot from a line of clergymen, his family had always felt he had a gnetism" that was referred to among them as "smartness."

To prepare for his new profession, Daniel traveled to London to study and stayed with some relatives, the Williams family. They welcomed him with open arms and made him feel quite at home. But Daniel's tiny Welsh parish was nothing like the thriving metropolis of London. London was fresh, new and full of ideas. While Welsh life was based on tradition, people in London were intellectually curious. Daniel was excited by this new atmosphere and used what little spare money he had to buy books. It was in this cosmopolitan environment that Daniel began to change. His mind was opened to new, different and unusual ideas, and some of them came from the Williamses.

The Williams family originally came from Penygonig on the Lleyn Peninsula, where the family had lived in a certain cottage for many generations. It was in that cottage, long ago, that the Williamses had come to possess a secret formula. Spanish sailors had been shipwrecked off the coast of Wales. The bedraggled sailors, close to death, were rescued by heroic locals. At the cottage, the sailors received food and medical attention from the women until their health returned. Out of their overwhelming gratitude, the Spanish sailors gave the Williams family the formula for a secret mixture that was said to cure skin cancer. The Williamses continued to use this knowledge even after relocating to London, and patients flocked to them. Patients who couldn't find relief from remedies provided by conventional medical practitioners came to the Williamses and received treatment using the secret Spanish formula, and they were healed. The established medical community criticized the Williamses for their practice, calling them charlatans, but the Williamses continued to treat patients, and the patients never ceased to come.

The Williams family housed and fed Daniel and apparently arranged for his classes and studies. Family members suggested that when his studies were complete he travel to the rural sections of Wales, for those were the people who would need to hear God's word the most.

While in London, Daniel developed a taste for reading diverse materials. One of the figures who most fascinated him in his reading was Dr. Franz Anton Mesmer, who introduced the idea of using magnets in curing sickness and disease. Daniel became interested in curing through the "laying on of hands." He began an intense study of the works and methods of Dr. Mesmer and wondered if he himself held a great healing power. Often Daniel had sensed a certain power inside himself and wondered if that power could be controlled and utilized to heal the sick and injured. He became interested in auras and discovered the mysterious symbol of "abracadabra." Daniel also became interested in telepathy. All of these new ideas changed him and his ambitions, and Daniel returned home to Wales with the intention of both preaching and healing the sick.

Upon his return, he was reunited with his sweetheart, Jaine. The two discovered that their love was just as strong and compelling as it had been, and they agreed to be married soon after Daniel had preached his first sermon. By that time, rumors had already spread of Daniel's strange powers, and his first sermon drew people from the surrounding countryside to the little chapel. The people were drawn by their own curiosity but left inspired by the sheer eloquence of Daniel's sermon. The consensus was that this fine young man was inspired by the spirit of God.

In May 1796, Daniel Roberts and Jaine Williams were wed in the little stone chapel, Jaine wearing a muslin dress decked with lace and Daniel wearing black. At the ceremony's conclusion, they rode away in a cart festooned with flowers for that special day. Their life together had finally begun. Daniel devoted much energy to his sermons and healing. His fame spread rapidly through the region. At times, Daniel felt he could see peoples' souls directly, and he occasionally felt uncomfortable with his newly discovered powers.

Though he had returned to his country village, Daniel was not the man he had been when he had left. His ideas had changed, he had polished his speaking and he was filled with novel ideas that must have seemed quite foreign to the Welsh villagers. Even his style of dressing had evolved as he dressed nattily in London fashion and wore buckles on his shoes. All these things did not go unnoticed in the tiny community. There was little doubt that Daniel Roberts was different.

In December 1799, Jaine gave birth to their first child, a daughter. Though Daniel had hoped for a son, he was charmed by the child, and they named her Mary, after his sister. She was a sweet, blue-eyed child that easily inspired parental love. In time, Jaine and Daniel's family would grow to include two daughters and a son named William. And also in time, Daniel grew more and more introverted, becoming distant from his work as a minister.

In the meantime, Daniel's brother, Robert, had married into the Williams family and moved to Penygonig to be near them. Robert would visit and tell Daniel of the wonderful cures resulting from the Williams family formula. In fact, according to Robert, many had been cured of their skin cancers through the secret formula, and the fame of the Williams family spread quickly. Daniel longed to heal the sick and to know the secret of the Williams family. Robert promised Daniel he would learn everything if he would agree to join the Williamses in their endeavor.

During the time Daniel had been preaching, he had felt his power increasing. When a man's sheep had been stolen, he preached the commandment "Thou shalt not steal" and let the spirit guide him in his oration. During the church service, a single man rose and left the chapel only to return a while later with the sheep slung over his shoulders. He deposited it at the altar. This and other incidents led to whispering among the people. Some began to fear his powers. He could see it in their faces and the way they avoided him. People still attended his sermons, but no one was quite convinced that he was using the spirit of God rather than the devil. Sometimes, during services, he would try to explain spiritual power to people, using examples from the Bible. However, people believed he was using magic.

Times were hard. Farmers suffered from low prices, and taxes were high. Many people could not find jobs, and those who worked often did not have enough. Those who had little had to provide for themselves before giving to the church, and in time, many small village churches were forced to close, unable to pay a cleric. Many men left Wales in search of employment in other lands, while others stayed, rioting and enacting violence to change their situations.

During these volatile times, Daniel and his family began staying with Robert in Penygonig, spending less and less time in their own parish. This experience offered new life to Daniel as he watched numerous patients come for the cure. Daniel was able to treat them with the secret Spanish formula. Many, who had given up hope after their experience with the medical profession, came to Daniel and the Williamses and walked away cancer free. Daniel was invigorated by the experience. He felt he had found his life's calling as a healer rather than as a preacher.

In time, Daniel decided that he and his family should leave Wales in search of a new life abroad. The family—as well as Daniel's siblings, Robert and Mary, and their respective families—departed from Cardiff, sailing on *The Hopewell* for America. Though the journey began smoothly, soon the passengers were consumed with fear as the ship experienced violently rough seas. Daniel acted as a spiritual leader on board *The Hopewell*, leading the group in Welsh hymns and prayer. However, illness spread on board the ship, and the food was inadequate. Overall, the trip was filled with hardship, but three months after embarking, *The Hopewell* arrived safely in New York.

Though Daniel had been to London, the newly arrived group was intimidated, disoriented and yet fascinated by the size and prosperity of New York. The group took care not to become lost among the maze of streets in New York City. As remarkable as the city seemed and as fascinating as it was, the group soon caught a boat up the Hudson to Albany. This trip proved serene and beautiful. The river was smooth, and the Robertses caught some of their first glimpses of America. They brought their own blankets for sleeping and ate their own food, and their spirits ran high with the excitement of the trip to their new home. By now, Dr. Roberts was not a young man. He was forty-one, had three children and was ready to build a new life for himself and his family. In Albany, all went ashore and stayed the night.

The journey was continued in keelboats, and the group poled its way to Utica. Rumor had it that the people in Steuben, the Welsh community where they would settle, were expecting him. There was talk of Dr. Roberts's tremendous power and perhaps even magic.

As it turned out, it was not only Dr. Roberts's magic that would impress them, for the year that they arrived became known as "The Year Without a Summer." It was a year of strange weather conditions that had resulted worldwide from the eruption of Mount Tambora in Indonesia. The winter in Steuben that year had been so mild that the townspeople hardly needed to heat their homes, but during the summer months, it seemed that winter had finally come. Ponds froze, and the weather was icy cold. Plants died and crops failed. Such weather had never been seen before. This mysterious reversal of summer and winter appeared to be a strange sign to the people of Steuben, and some speculated it foreshadowed the arrival of the powerful magician and healer, Daniel Roberts.

At last they arrived at *Tě Coch*, or Red House. This was a small farmhouse owned by Evan Evans and his Welsh family who were to receive the travelers in their new country. Soon enough, Dr. Roberts's family had made a home nearby. As the local Welsh had already known of his coming, many people came seeking cures, having heard so much of his healing powers. In fact, there was so much traffic in and out of the Robertses' home that Dr. Roberts had to construct a window right next to his front door where he could fill prescriptions for people from the inside. Perhaps this was the first walk-up pharmacy window in America. People did not just come by to pick up a cure, however. Some patients were quite ill. These patients were housed in whatever spare rooms the Robertses or their neighbors had available.

While nearby residents were often grateful for the miraculous medical care they and their families were receiving, they also began to feel uncomfortable when strange phenomenon began to occur. Some felt that invisible spirits inhabited the area surrounding the doctor. These spirits seemed to aid Roberts in locating thieves or eliciting confessions from the guilty.

Incidents, such as one involving a fleece that had been laid to dry on the grass ended up arranged in the treetops, set residents on edge. Dr. Roberts also demonstrated telepathic abilities, such as the time he told Jaine guests would arrive and described their wagon. Dr. Roberts used fear to detect thieves. In one instance, he had some men sit in a circle. After declaring that one of them had stolen a local man's harness, he told them to all stand up except for the thief. If the one who had stolen the harness were to stand, Dr. Roberts warned, he would fall dead instantaneously. All but one stood up.

One time, Dr. Roberts had to travel to the North Country. There, he stayed at an inn for the night, and the innkeeper overcharged him. To change his ways, Dr. Roberts wrote a Latin symbol on the mantel using chalk. He was sure the innkeeper would see it, though he would unlikely be able to read the Latin. Dr. Roberts left, but soon afterward, he turned to find a runner approaching him, begging him to return to the inn. He did, and the staff asked him to erase the symbol, for it seems the owner of the inn and the maid were cast under a spell where they could not stop dancing. Dr. Roberts agreed, but only if they were to promise never to overcharge again. The promise was made. The sign was erased, and all returned to normal.

On another occasion, Dr. Roberts and his brother were in the barn. They drew a circle around themselves and began to read from magic books. Dark figures materialized in the barn, and a great pounding was heard on the roof, but the two men remained protected within their magic circle. As incidents like this continued, the townspeople became more fearful and suspicious. Where they once had welcomed Roberts with open arms, they now felt anxious with him near.

One remarkable incident demands retelling. One night, after returning from a medical call, he passed Capel Ucha and noticed a man with a gun waiting in the darkness. These men were standing guard at the cemetery, watching for grave robbers—medical students from Pineview Medical School nearby, who had been snatching the bodies of the dead from the graveyard. Not long before that night, a young girl's corpse had been exhumed and taken. The guards were bent on retrieving her.

Dr. Daniels rode with the group to Pineview Medical School, and they pounded on the door. There was nothing but silence on the other side. Finally, a faculty member opened the door. The crowd demanded the body of the girl, but the faculty member denied knowledge of her. After some shouting back and forth, the group of vigilantes fired a shot at the school , and at last, the faculty member admitted that the girl's body was in the dissecting room. They retrieved her and then returned her body to its proper resting place.

The group demanded and received a signed statement from the president of the school that no more bodies would be stolen. The president's statement was added to the medical school's charter, and the anatomy professor was forced to resign. Such were some of the strange occurrences in early Steuben, what some might today call a quiet town.

With time, the religious beliefs of the people of Steuben took a turn. The Revivalist movement was soon afoot. Drink was said to be a brew of the devil. Even women who wore simple embellishments were criticized. Dr. Roberts and his family disagreed with these newly enforced restrictions. They no longer attended church, preferring to study the Bible in their own fashion instead. One day, however, a fight broke out between the deacon's son and William, Dr. Roberts's son. The deacon's son had accused Dr. Roberts of being satanic and a practitioner of black magic. A crowd gathered to watch the two boys as they punched each other and shouted insults. Soon, however, the sun vanished, and an enormous black cloud formed over Capel Ucha Hill. A local man cried out a warning and ran to his wagon to get the horses into the barn before the storm arrived. Others also fled, and the two boys continued their fight alone. But a storm was not coming. The large black cloud that was descending on Steuben moved quickly, in a way that was strange for clouds. As it approached, the townspeople realized that it was not a cloud but millions of grasshoppers. Some said it was the work of God. Whatever its origin, the grasshoppers stripped the crops from the fields and the leaves from the trees. Not a plant was left whole when it was over. Some said that it was the Lord's way of punishing the intemperate and gossips, and there came a call for all sinners to repent and return to the ways of God. Furthermore, horrible news arrived in Steuben. The pastor, who had gone to Albany to visit family, had been murdered, and his body was found in the Hudson River. It appeared he had been robbed. This vacancy was soon filled with a pro-temperance minister. Soon after, the store mysteriously burned down. People were in an explosive state.

Not long after, a mob of people noisily approached the house. Daniel went to see what they wanted. They were sure Dr. Roberts was the cause of a great curse that had fallen upon Steuben, and they demanded he surrender his books of magic so they might be burned. Dr. Roberts looked at the men, went inside and returned with four leather-bound books. He surrendered them to the mob, saying, "Do with them what you wish! And may God have mercy on your souls!" Looking down at the books, the leader of the mob realized he was holding four Welsh Bibles. Ashamed, the mob turned away.

During a time when his brother had been ill, Dr. Roberts cared for him. The doctor suffered from lack of sleep and mounted his horse to ride homeward. However, as he rode, a rabbit ran in front of his horse. The horse jumped, throwing Dr. Roberts onto the creek bank before running off. It eventually returned home, leaving Dr. Roberts in the creek with multiple injuries. When the horse returned without its rider, Evan Evans searched for him and brought him home so that he could be nursed back to health, but his injuries were too great, and he did not recover. Dr. Daniel Roberts died in September of 1820.

He was buried in the cemetery by Capel Ucha. The gathering was the largest anyone could recall. Strangely, the patients continued to come to the witch doctor's house. Jaine never moved his possessions, and the house remained as it had when he was living. Even his coat and hat remained by the door. It was as if he never left.

IROQUOIS WITCHCRAFT

Both men and women among the Iroquois could be considered witches. Iroquois witchcraft had nothing to do with a belief in or alliance with the devil. Rather, an Iroquois witch was someone who practiced evil magic and brought ill fortune upon those around him. Iroquois witches were thought to hold a variety of supernatural powers, which included such phenomena as turning into animals. It was difficult sometimes for people to know if an animal was a witch in another form. At other times, it was obvious, such as in the case of a dog or buffalo streaming fire from its mouth and nostrils. There were instances where a witch would be identified when an animal was seen transforming into human form or visa versa.

Perhaps a witch's most dreaded skill was his or her ability to inflict disease on an individual or a group of people. Early Jesuits encountered Iroquois, and being foreigners, the Jesuits often carried diseases to which the Iroquois were not immune. Many times, soon after making contact with a group of Iroquois, disease would spread through the Iroquois' ranks, causing much suffering and often resulting in death. For this reason, the Jesuit missionaries were often accused of witchcraft of the most horrific nature. The Iroquois believed that a witch could kill or sicken people or animals just by pointing a finger at them.

Oftentimes when an Iroquois fell ill, he or she would be treated with medicinal plant remedies. If none of the treatments worked, then it was presumed that there was a supernatural cause. Perhaps the diseased person was the holder of a charm and had neglected to perform the proper ceremony in a timely fashion. Perhaps the patient was the victim of a familial ghost or, as often was the case, the person could have been bewitched. Sometimes the witch was apparent (for instance, if someone had been seen pointing at the person before he or she became ill), but some sort of divination was often necessary to determine who had caused the malady. Some Iroquois were said to have carried crystals in their noses or mouths and would draw them forth and place the crystals in gourds filled with water. The image of the bewitcher would then appear to the diviner, and the crystal could then be used in curing the sick individual. Still, other curers would place roots or herbs in a pot of water and boil them, and a shaman would then cover his head with a blanket and peer into the pot of water to see who the witch was who was causing the illness at hand.

As one of the frequent effects of bewitchment was illness (and sometimes death), witchcraft was not welcome among the Iroquois. When witches were discovered, they were simply executed. There appeared to be no due process involved. Also, it was possible for witches to be in one place in body and somewhere else in spirit. Because of that, it was impossible for an accused witch to offer a good alibi.

The Screech Owl Witch

Once there was a man whose brother had fallen ill, and he suspected the cause was witchcraft. However, he had no idea who the witch might be, as witches were secretive about their evil craft. The young man did not know where he could find the witches, so he told an old woman that he wished to become a witch himself.

"Is that so?" she asked. "Then you must prove that. Go home and point your finger at your sister. She will be taken ill, and in time, she will die."

The man went to his sister and told her all that had happened. They agreed that she would pretend to be ill and let everyone know it.

At last, the night arrived when the witches were to meet. The young man walked with the old woman to the place in the dark, but as he walked, he made sure he left a trail of leaves and broken branches to mark the way. Suddenly, the old woman was transformed into an enormous panther, and she sprang into a nearby tree, hissing menacingly at the man. She swatted toward him with her great paw and bared her teeth. The man was terrified, but he was determined not to show his fear. When the woman became herself again, she asked him if he had been afraid. "Oh no," replied the man, "I was not afraid. My hope is that I can become a panther myself." The two of them continued on until they reached a clearing where the witches were gathered around a fire.

It was a strange scene that the man beheld. There, hanging over the fire, was the tiniest cauldron. A number of snakes were suspended above it, their blood dribbling down into the awaiting cauldron below. Each witch drank from the tiny cauldron of blood, but the young man only pretended to drink. Old and young men and women surrounded the fire, many of whom the man recognized. But the familiar faces suddenly took new forms as the witches became various animals, such as foxes, panthers, owls, wolves and hawks. They did strange things and repeatedly asked the young man what he would like to be. He finally answered that he would like to be a screech owl, and they gave him the head of a screech owl and told him to put it on later. They said that he would fly while wearing it. He flapped his arms and made the screeching cry of the owl, and the witches told him he would make a fine owl.

At last, the meeting broke up, and the witches left, wandering off in their various animal forms. The young man decided to put on the head of the screech owl to see if he could really fly. As soon as he was wearing the owl head, he lost all control of himself and began to fly. He flew to his brother's house, and all those present were terrified when they heard the strange screeching of the owl outside (the owl is considered an ill omen among the Iroquois). The young man then removed the head and came inside. He pointed at the dog, which became ill and eventually died.

The witches visited his sister who was pretending to be ill, and all of them wished her well as though they had nothing to do with her supposed illness.

The next day, the young man went to the warriors and told them what he had witnessed. That night, the warriors followed the young man along the path he had marked. When they arrived at the clearing, the witches' meeting had begun, and they could hear the witches making speeches. As they drew close, they could hear the words of the speaker. He said the Good Spirit would amply reward the witches if they killed any people because the people they killed may be saved from ill fortune or evil.

At that moment, the young man gave a sign to the warriors, and they rushed in and killed all the witches.

CHAPTER TWO
IROQUOIS MYSTICAL TRADITIONS

DREAMS

No one truly understands the nature of dreams. Throughout history and among different cultures, people have had different ideas of what dreams mean. In modern American society, some believe that dreams are bits and pieces of experiences and thoughts we have had during the day and that our subconscious strings these ideas together, forming dreams that help commit these ideas and experiences to long-term memory. Others believe dreams indicate unresolved conflicts or issues that we might have within ourselves. In certain cultures, dreams are thought to be prophetic; what we see in dreams is what will be so. To a large extent, this was also a core belief of the Iroquois. If you dreamed something, then it was said that it would come true as it was thought to be the desire of the Great Spirit. This concept became quite important in the life of General William Johnson, for whom the city of Johnstown is named.

Sir William Johnson's Dreamland

General William Johnson (c. 1715–1774) became very close to the Iroquois, and unlike many, took the time to learn their language. He hunted and fished with the native people, traded with them and invited them to his home. He grew very close to Joseph Brant, the Mohawk chief, and at one point, Johnson was formally adopted by the Mohawk Indian tribe.

Occasionally, Johnson would hold festivities at his home that were rather elaborate, especially in the eyes of the Iroquois, who made their home in the

Mezzotint by Charles Spooner depicting Sir William Johnson, major general of the English forces in America. *Courtesy of the Library of Congress.*

woodlands. On one occasion, Johnson entertained guests for several days, and one of his guests was a Mohawk named Soiengarahta, known to English speakers as King Hendrick. It was said that Hendrick wandered from room to room in Johnson's home, admiring his fine things, possessions that must have seemed quite different from those of an Iroquois. In one room he entered, he spotted a scarlet coat embroidered in magnificent gold placed over the back of a chair. Johnson had only recently received the garment from England.

King Hendrick, fascinated by the coat's beauty, returned daily to gaze upon it. On the third and final day, he exchanged pleasantries with Johnson and then said, "Brother, last night I had a dream."

"Indeed!" answered Johnson. "Then tell us what it was about."

"Brother," Hendrick replied, "I dreamed that the beautiful coat was mine."

"Then brother, it is yours!" Johnson said.

A joyful and exuberant Hendrick took the prized coat and disappeared. He was seen soon after wearing the magnificent red and gold coat. Not long after this incident, Johnson decided to host yet another party as a

The Brave old Hendrick, the Great Sachem or Chief of the Mohawk Indians. Courtesy of the Library of Congress.

reward for his officers, and Hendrick, among many others, was invited to join him and his guests. The party was lavish, and the guests stayed late at Johnson's home.

The next day, Johnson awoke, dressed himself and went to call upon Hendrick. He asked the Mohawk how he had slept after his night at the party.

"Brother," Johnson said, "I had an extraordinary dream last night."

"And what did you dream, brother?" asked King Hendrick.

Johnson slowly spoke and expanded his arms into a great arc before him. "I dreamed all these lands were mine."

Hendrick looked at Johnson, stunned by the magnitude of the request. The woodland Johnson spoke of was estimated by some to be roughly 100,000 acres. Others sources say it was 60,000 acres. Nonetheless, this was the home of Hendrick's people, and it was difficult for the Mohawk to understand how the Great Spirit could prefer Johnson to own this land rather than the Iroquois. Still, if it were a dream, then the Great Spirit had decreed this to be. It must be so. Hendrick saw no other option but to pass ownership to Johnson.

After a long silence, Hendrick spoke. "The land is yours. But you, my brother, must not dream again."

This incredible expanse of land became known as "The Dream Land" and lies north of the Mohawk River, part of what is now known as Herkimer County.

The Otherworldly Dream of Handsome Lake

"The Code of Handsome Lake" has been passed down among the Iroquois for generations in the oral tradition. Handsome Lake was an Iroquois who was born around 1735 and lived in the Seneca community near the Allegheny River. His message, however, influenced the religious beliefs of the entire Iroquois people. Handsome Lake had developed a severe drinking problem, which was not uncommon among the Indians. (Prior to European colonization, Native Americans had not been exposed to alcohol and may not have developed an ability to metabolize it as well as Europeans. Some early accounts of the Iroquois describe addiction to alcohol and drunkenness.) Alcoholism seemed to consume Handsome Lake's life.

On June 15, 1799, according to Iroquois accounts, the Creator spoke to Handsome Lake through a vision or a dream. Handsome Lake had become very ill. In fact, he had been ill for four years, and it was uncertain how long he would survive. He was staying with his half-brother, Cornplanter, at the time. (Cornplanter, a Seneca chief who fought in the French and Indian War and on the side of the British in the American Revolution, was instrumental in welcoming the Quakers to Seneca lands to open schools.) As Handsome Lake lay resting, he began to think about the Creator, hoping that perhaps He would allow Handsome Lake to recover to health. But these thoughts were short-lived, and he resigned himself to the Creator, imagining his time was near.

Then, Handsome Lake heard a voice call him from outside. He rose and walked outdoors, stumbling over the threshold, and was met by three men who steadied him. Each of the men stood holding a berry bush filled with berries. They told him that he would live until summer to see the berries ripen on the bush once again. Handsome Lake carefully ate a berry from each of the three bushes and was told the berries would bring him back his health. The men explained to him that the Creator saw the drunkenness of his people and that these ways were not good. The Creator was displeased. Handsome Lake had been made sick to abstain from drink so that he might ponder the Creator. He was told a fourth personage was yet to come.

When that personage did arrive, Handsome Lake believed that he was speaking to the Creator himself. (Handsome Lake's grandson believed the fourth personage was also a messenger of the Creator, and not the Creator himself.) He told Handsome Lake that he did, indeed, pity him and intended to take him away.

When Handsome Lake awoke, he told Cornplanter that he would soon be seeing his son and Cornplanter's daughter, both of whom had already died. Handsome Lake's arms and legs then grew cold. He spent the next seven hours in a trance. A man wearing clothes the color of the sky and carrying a quiver of arrows and a bow appeared to him and brought him to see both his son and his niece. Handsome Lake's son told him that he was dissatisfied that his own son was not caring for Handsome Lake in his time of need. Handsome Lake's niece said that she was very disturbed about the heated arguments that Handsome Lake and her brother would frequently have.

The guide then spoke to Handsome Lake and admonished him to give up alcohol. The two of them stood at the bank of a river, and as he watched, Handsome Lake could see many canoes loaded with barrels of whiskey, and he saw an ugly fellow, identified to him as the "Evil-minded," who constantly created problems and disturbances.

Handsome Lake was told that the messengers have always watched over the Creator's people and that they were well aware of the happenings of men. Handsome Lake was at once transported into the sky where he viewed those on Earth below. As Handsome Lake looked down, he saw a multitude of people, out of which a tattered man wearing ragged clothes emerged. He was a filthy man and obviously very poor and unhappy. The messengers told Handsome Lake that this man was a drunkard. Firewater had brought him to this state. Next, Handsome Lake saw a woman who was constantly hiding her belongings. The messengers explained the woman was inhospitable and selfish. This kind of woman would never progress to heaven. Finally, a man carrying some meat appeared. The man went to each of those assembled below and gave each a piece. That man, he was told, was blessed for his kindness and hospitality as he lived in the spirit the Creator intended.

Streams of flowing blood appeared to Handsome Lake. This, he was told, would be the result if the use of alcohol was not stopped among the people. Brothers and friends both would begin to fight and kill each other. There would be violence and murder. Now Handsome Lake's vision swept toward the East, and he watched as countless distilleries appeared until the shining light of the sun was completely shaded from view. Handsome Lake was disgusted and horrified at the scene. Next, he saw what appeared to be a fine house but was told it was a prison filled with whips and ropes. This is where the Iroquois drinkers would be confined by white men. He then watched different groups of individuals. Those drinking were unruly and violent, while those who did not consume alcohol listened, were peaceful and remembered the Creator. Those people pleased the Great Spirit, but the drinkers displeased him and brought ruin upon their own lives. Alcohol caused many people to die prematurely. This was not what the Creator had intended.

In this vision, Handsome Lake saw two places unknown to the Iroquois at the time. One was a Native American version of heaven; the other was the House of Torment, where the Evil-minded made his abode.

When an Iroquois dies, as Handsome Lake later told his people, his spirit travels on a path skyward, and at a certain point in the sky, there is a fork. The Iroquois's spirit would find two gatekeepers there, one of them representing the Creator and all that is good, and the other representing the Evil-minded. If the spirit of the deceased had lived a goodly life and followed the Code, he or she was allowed to progress on the straight path that led to the abode of the Creator. This path was infrequently used, so grass could grow underfoot. One could see a most brilliant light shining in the distance, and eventually, one could find a cold spring where the traveler could relax and refresh for a time on his journey. After resuming the trip, the deceased would find himself passing through a vast land of fairies and then the good-hearted Iroquois would find himself in heaven. The light was stunning, for its brilliance was magnificent, unlike any light on earth. The land abounded with berries and fruits of every variety. Even a single berry would satisfy the appetite, for they were large and bountiful. The air smelled sweet. The afterlife of one who entered heaven was a life of leisure, pleasure and recreation. Evil never entered the confines of this sacred space, and each person lived in harmony with others. Families might find each other beyond death here, but no white man might step foot in this utopia. Only one was seen nearby. Just outside the perimeter of this heavenly abode, Handsome Lake said, lies a fort, and in that fort, George Washington could be seen. Washington, Handsome Lake was told, was the only white man ever to leave the earth as he had been good to the Iroquois during and after the times of the Revolutionary War, offering protection to the Iroquois people. He did not exterminate the Indians, but rather let them survive. Because of this, he survives eternally outside the walls of heaven, but as he is a white man, he would never be allowed to see the Great Spirit. Handsome Lake was assured that Washington was content with his solitude. All Iroquois who headed to that sacred place pass him on their great journey, but none speak to him, nor does he speak to them. Each recognizes the other in respectful silence. That is the path and destination of a good Iroquois.

Most, however, do not take that road. At the fork, they are turned aside by the sentry to another place, the abode of the Evil-minded, known also as the House of Torment. Some Iroquois who have only erred in small, insubstantial ways only go there on a temporary basis, for a day or a few days (according to lore, a day in that land is equal to a year on our earth). Then they are rerouted onto the straight path and spend the rest of eternity in the heavenly Indian abode. Others, however, who have committed major transgressions, are sent to the House of Torment for all eternity.

In his vision, Handsome saw various scenes of the House of Torment. First, he was shown a soot-encrusted mansion next to a smaller building. One of the four messengers who accompanied Handsome Lake pointed at the building with a rod, and remarkably, the rooftop levitated away, revealing many rooms within. Inside, Handsome Lake saw a tired, worn man with dark, sunken eyes, who had been a drunk during his life. The man stared blankly at the ground. He had been a drunk during his life. A moment later, the Evil-minded came and dipped a scoop deep into a cauldron containing a liquid so hot that one could sense the heat from it. He told the man to drink it, reminding him that it is what the man loved best. The pathetic man drank, and steam and fire arose from his mouth. Though the suffering man screamed for mercy, the Evil-minded only told him to sing and be happy as he had in his earthly life after drinking firewater.

Next, the Evil-minded brought forth a couple who had been married in life. The Evil-minded told them to do what they loved best, and they began to argue and fight. They screamed and fought so violently until they could no longer see or speak. This was their punishment.

The Evil-minded then had a witch brought forth. He threw her into a giant cauldron of boiling water, and Handsome Lake could barely bring himself to listen to the sound of her tormented howls as she begged to be removed. The Evil-minded then removed her from the cauldron and plunged her instead into a cauldron of freezing water. Again, the woman howled and screamed unabatedly.

The Evil-minded now brought a man into the room who had lived his life as a wife-beater. Before him stood a burning hot statue of a woman, and the man was told to do what he did during his life. He struck the statue with all his might, and his arm was consumed by fire.

An emaciated woman was brought before the Evil-minded. Her crime upon earth had been selling alcohol to the Indians. Her punishment was to have all the meat eaten off her arms and hands until only bone protruded.

In another room, Handsome saw an old friend his. His name was Farmer's Brother. He was very busy with the task of removing sand one grain at a time. He worked unceasingly, but the height of the sand pile did not change. His crime upon earth had been selling land, but the Creator did not make land to be sold as a commodity.

Outside the house was some land that was filled with all manner of weeds that surrounded a corn crop. Women worked in the field cutting the weeds, but the weeds grew faster than the women could cut. These, Handsome Lake was told, were lazy women.

The messenger told Handsome Lake that there was more to see but that their time was limited. He then told Handsome Lake the following: People are social animals, and so, you must exercise hospitality when someone visits you. People should never steal. Always be kind and generous to the old and those who cannot help themselves. Only mourn the dead for ten days rather than the customary year and express respect for the deceased.

Before Handsome Lake's dream ended, he was told of the splendor of the Great Spirit. One day, the messenger said, the Great Spirit will tell the keeper of the clouds to stop his labors. The keeper of the brooks and springs will also cease, and the sun will no longer shine. A great darkness will envelop the earth. Then, the horrible monsters and poisonous creatures created by the Evil-minded will come forth and pursue wicked men. This is the way it will end. Before this happens, however, the Great Spirit will bring the good people back to him, and they will be protected.

As promised, Handsome Lake did live to see the berries ripen, and he told his people that the four messengers had given him a divine order to preach what he had learned to them to save the Creator's people from their current path of degradation. The things that had been revealed to him became known as "The Code of Handsome Lake," (and is sometimes called "The Good Message") and that moral code changed the way of life for many. The Code of Handsome Lake was an oral tradition, retold on countless occasions over the generations. It was recited after his death by his grandson. In time, it became Iroquois tradition to recite the code in the long house every other year (worship was traditionally confined to the hours before noon). The practice would occupy several morning sessions.

Author's note: In the Iroquois story of creation, there were two brothers: one was the Creator and the other was the Evil-minded. While it is tempting to think of this brother as the devil, the Evil-minded has a legitimate place in

Iroquois mythology prior to the natives' introduction to Christianity. This is not to suggest that Handsome Lake was not influenced in his dream by Christian concepts of Heaven and Hell, to which he had been exposed through Quaker religious influences.

THE RELIGIOUS USE OF TOBACCO

Today the use of tobacco in its many forms seems ubiquitous. It is used throughout the world, and the sight of smokers is a common one in everyone's experience. However, despite tobacco's pervasiveness, many people have little knowledge about its origin. Tobacco was initially cultivated by the Native Americans, and upon contact with Europeans, tobacco spread rapidly throughout the world. Tobacco was used as a religious or spiritual tool by the Iroquois and other native New World peoples (although writings of early Jesuits suggest that it was also used secularly by Native Americans).

People today have great concerns over smoking, and New York State banned smoking in public spaces on July 24, 2003, due to health concerns. Despite the emphasis on smoking bans in recent decades, there have been, in actuality, warnings about the health effects of smoking tobacco since 1602. A pamphlet titled "Worke of Chimney Sweeps or A Warning for Tabacconists [*sic*]" was published in England, warning readers that tobacco evaporated unctuous and radical moistures. This, the anonymous author had gleaned, resulted from tobacco's use treating gonorrhea.

Perhaps the first smoking ban was set in place in 1575 in Mexico, when the Roman Catholic Church banned smoking in churches in the Spanish colonies. Massachusetts, ever the progressive state, or then colony as it were, banned smoking in public places in 1632. Smoking bans and health warnings, therefore, are nothing new. Columbus was given tobacco as one of several gifts upon entering the New World. However, he discarded them, not understanding the purpose of the dried leaves. Once Europeans witnessed and perhaps experienced smoking, however, tobacco use rapidly spread worldwide. It was always controversial, and there have been numerous and sundry bans of it throughout the world for various reasons, including the fire hazard it posed, health risks and rudeness of smoking in public.

It is believed that by 1 CE, few places in the Americas did *not* have tobacco. The Iroquois describe the origin of tobacco in their creation myth. When Sky Woman fell from Sky World to the watery world below, the animals attempted to save her. At last, Turtle was able to serve as a support, and the animals brought dirt from deep beneath the water to cover the Turtle's back so that Sky Woman had a place to stand. Sky Woman arrived on this newly formed earth pregnant and gave birth to a daughter, who was later courted by the animals. She at last was wed to Turtle, who gave her two twin sons: a good son and an evil one. The good son was born naturally, and the evil one tore his way out of his mother, taking her life. When the twins buried their mother, the three sisters—corn, beans and squash—sprung from her body. Tobacco grew from her heart as a great gift from the Creator that would serve as a way for people to communicate with and give thanks to the Creator. Tobacco, then, was sacred to the Iroquois and other Indians. Its use was ritualistic, and before white man arrived in the New World, tobacco was considered a great gift of the Creator, not a vice.

Tobacco was used as a vehicle of prayer. It was thought the smoke from burning tobacco would carry the people's prayers to the Creator himself. To smoke the tobacco, a pipe was used. The pipe was often made of clay and sometimes elaborately decorated, perhaps with clan symbols. The pipe itself was symbolic. The bowl of the pipe was said to represent the head, while the handle represented the spine. The joint where the handle connects to the pipe was considered the breath of the pipe. The pipe and tobacco were used by the Iroquois and other native peoples in a variety of religious ceremonies. They were also used to seal pacts and form friendships. Smoking was a form of both prayer and meditation.

Tobacco was probably not cultivated by women but by men, as it was used for ceremonial and religious purposes. Tobacco was grown in small gardens that were likely separate from the food gardens. The type of tobacco historically grown by Iroquois was *Nicotiana rustica* and is considered a member of the solanaceae family, commonly known as nightshades. The tobacco was far more potent than the modern tobacco that is sold today. It had the potential for being toxic. Seed for *Nicotiana rustica* is still available commercially today for home gardening. Victory Seed Company offers a description of the plant as having originated in Mexico, but it was cultivated across North America for ceremonial purposes. Its toxicity is such that it was used as an arrow poison in Mexico. Some members of the nightshade family are also known for their hallucinogenic effects, and some users report such experiences. Furthermore, smoke is an effective means to introduce nicotine into the brain. It is more rapid than an intravenous injection. Standard cigarettes made with modern cultivated tobacco are usually considered to be stimulants. Interestingly, smoking *Nicotiana rustica* has a reverse effect, as small quantities of nicotine stimulate the brain and large amounts act as

An Iroquois log cabin, originally from the Onondaga Reservation, is now on the Oneida Nation Territory at the Shako:wi Cultural Center. This is the style of homes that were used by the Iroquois after they ceased to live in long houses. *Photo courtesy of the author.*

a depressant. Overdoses can cause death to the user. (Also worthy of note, many shamans from South American native societies would consume tobacco to bring themselves into a comatose state, from which they would recover.)

Nicotiana rustica contains three to nine times the concentration of nicotine as a modern commercial tobacco. Smoking native tobacco (using a pipe) can reportedly cause the user to suffer such effects as falling asleep while walking, falling into a deep meditative state, vomiting, erratic mood swings, out-of-body experiences, euphoria and experiencing things in the spirit world, as well as changes in perception of sights and sounds. However, not all users report hallucinogenic effects.

There is evidence of emphysema-like symptoms in historical Native American families. The Farmers' Museum in Cooperstown has an example of an Iroquois single family home on the hill behind the main grounds of the museum. These homes were common after the Iroquois ceased living together in long houses. An example of that type of home is shown on above. The home is two stories high but no bigger than a modern small room. Numerous members of an extended family, perhaps as many as fifteen people, would live inside this simple structure. Often an elder would sleep in a small bed by the fireplace downstairs. The bed is said to be short, not because the Iroquois were particularly short, but because older people often had to sleep sitting up slightly due to a lung condition that was common. Though lung problems may have developed in men from smoking, elder Iroquois women were more likely to have smoke exposure from a cooking fire that may have led to lung maladies. In Iroquois society, the men smoked, but the women did not.

CHAPTER THREE

MONSTERS, FAIRIES AND OTHER BEINGS

The tales in this chapter include a variety of the many monsters, fairies, beasts and other weird and exotic creatures that either currently dwell in this vast and diverse patch of land we call Central New York or creatures who have inhabited this region in the past according to local lore. Many of those mentioned seem to possess some amount of magical ability or power. All of them are worth discussing, and a few of them are still generating complaints from people. Among the variety of creatures included in this section are stone giants, flying heads, Bigfoot, lake monsters, Little People and the Ro-tay-yo, or giant mosquito, as well as an ancient mummy. This region was inhabited by such a wide variety of magical or otherwise strange beings that its a wonder people managed to get by at all. A number of the creatures mentioned were far from benign, and it behooved the wise man to just lay low, cultivate some form of powerful counter magic or develop a very sharp wit. Even today, when walking in the woods, people still sometimes feel the need to take an occasional quick glance behind, because you never know...

STONE GIANTS

There were originally five Iroquois nations: the Oneida, the Onondaga, the Mohawk, the Seneca and the Cayuga. In 1722, the Tuscaroras were added. The Tuscaroras were an Iroquoian tribe that migrated northward from what is today North Carolina and were sponsored by the Oneidas. The Tuscaroras shared the Oneida Indians' land before gaining their own. The Iroquois nations were troubled by the stone giants, but it appears, according to lore, that the stone giants plagued the Tuscaroras even before their relocation north to New York. Though the stone giants originated far from here, they met their end on Onondaga land.

The Origins of the Stone Giants

There was a family that was traveling on the east side of the Mississippi River. When they arrived at the river's bank, they had found a huge vine and used it to cross the river. It's uncertain whether they crossed by swinging over the river or somehow used the vine as a bridge by hanging from it, but after a portion of the family had crossed, the vine broke, leaving the majority of the family on the eastern bank. Those who did not manage to cross the great river realized that they had no way to rejoin their family, and they migrated away and soon lost knowledge of their culture and their ways. They became wild and began to eat raw meat and cannibalize people. They also adopted the peculiar custom of rolling in the sand to form a hard coating on their skins, which deflected the arrows of the Tuscaroras. This is how they came to be called "stone giants." These stone giants lived like vagrants, migrating from place to place and primarily living in wooded terrain.

Skunny-Wundy

There was once a man named Skunny-Wundy, and though he did not seem physically extraordinary in any way, everyone knew of him, because Skunny-Wundy never ceased to boast about his bravery and his strength. Those around him wished he would say less and do more, but no one liked to confront him on this matter since Skunny-Wundy was known as a trickster. Those who spoke against him soon found themselves the butt of a practical joke. Still, it was hard to be around him, listening to him go on and on about his great deeds and what great feats he planned to accomplish.

Now many people think times were good back in those days, but back then, many monsters roamed the earth, people were terrorized by flying heads, human-headed bears and a wide assortment of other creatures, but the thing that frightened people the most were the stone giants. After all, the giants were big and had magical powers, pointy heads and skin like rock. Worst of all, they loved to eat people. Everybody back in those days knew about the stone giants, and just the thought of them sent a chill through the spine of even the bravest of warriors.

One day, as Skunny-Wundy was bragging about himself, an old sachem asked him if he was afraid of the stone giants. "Stone giants?" cried Skunny-Wundy. "Why should I fear them? I am the bravest, the greatest, and the most powerful of warriors! It is the stone giants that should fear me!" And on Skunny-Wundy went, talking about himself until he realized no one was listening. In fact, everyone had quietly slipped away into the council house while he was bragging.

He stood there for some time, wondering why everybody had gone, and then watched as they left the council house. They all stood around him, and the sachem announced. "We have understood how brave you are, and we have decided to give you the chance to prove yourself! Skunny-Wundy, you should celebrate this opportunity."

For the first time, Skunny-Wundy felt a little nervous and frightened as the whole village gathered around him. "And what exactly will I be doing to prove myself?" he asked.

The old sachem smiled and told Skunny-Wundy that the village had decided that he should be the one to fight the stone giants since he was so brave.

"Oh," said Skunny-Wundy, "Well, that will be no problem at all since I am such a powerful warrior. I suspect the stone giants will run when they see me approach. I am not sure where they are anyway."

"In fact," said the old man, "there is a stone giant just outside the village standing on the other side of the river. We saw him standing there and told him he should run for his life from you, since you are such a powerful warrior, Skunny-Wundy, but he was only angered by the message and has promised to wait for you."

Skunny-Wundy was terrified inside, but with the whole village watching him, he could not show it. Nor could he avoid the giant because he knew he would never live that down, especially after all he had said and all the tricks he had played on people over the years.

"Good then," he said. "I will meet him. I am sure he will run in fear when he sees me and my mighty tomahawk." And off he strode, but as soon as Skunny-Wundy slipped behind the nearest trees, he began to walk very slowly, wondering how he could possibly overcome an enemy so great.

"If I try to shoot the giant with my arrows, the arrows will simply bounce off his stone skin. If I pelt the giant with rocks, he could pick up the stones and eat them like tasty morsels. My weapons are useless against him."

Skunny-Wundy knew that with such a powerful enemy, he could not win by fighting or with his weapons. The only true weapon he had to defeat the stone giant would be his wit. Skunny-Wundy would need to trick the giant.

Just then, Skunny-Wundy heard a great and strange sound. It was like the wind in the midst of a hurricane, and it was like a great pounding. *Swish* BOOM! *Swish* BOOM! *Swish* BOOM! Terrified inside, Skunny-Wundy slipped his head out from behind the tree where he was hiding and peered across the creek. There stood the stone giant, tall as two men and angry as an unruly mob. The giant had grabbed a tree and, with one thrust of its great arm, had dislodged the tree from the soil by the creek. He shook the tree over his head and beat it on the ground as if it were an enormous drumstick. He sang (or bellowed, rather) a horrifying war song, and his voice was so loud that Skunny-Wundy almost covered his ears.

Skunny-Wundy was terrified and decided to run. He cared little at that point if he would be the laughing stock of the village for the rest of his life. At least, perhaps, he would have a life. So he turned carefully and began to tiptoe away back toward the village. But the giant discovered him.

"Arrgh! Who comes my way?" the giant shouted. "Is it Skunny-Wundy who claims to be such a great warrior he can defeat even me, the mighty stone giant? Ha ha! No one defeats a stone giant!"

Skunny-Wundy knew he could not escape, so he would have to face the giant. He stepped out from behind the tree where he was hiding and boldly hollered in his deepest voice, "Yes, it is me, the great warrior Skunny-Wundy! Come here to this side of the creek and fight me. It will be your last fight, stone giant!"

The giant, with the tree still in his great hand, headed to the creek and began to wade across. The creek was deep, and before he was halfway across, the giant disappeared beneath the surface of the water. When he did, Skunny-Wundy wasted no time in running to a shallow place in the creek and quickly waded to the other side.

When the giant emerged from the water, he looked around and spotted Skunny-Wundy on the other side of the creek. "What are you doing over there, you coward?!" he shouted.

"I am just waiting for you to come over to fight me!" Skunny-Wundy cried. "You must have become turned around when you were under water. I am still waiting for you to come over here."

"ARRRH!" the giant yelled, and he rushed back into the water. Once again, as soon as the giant vanished beneath the water, a terrified Skunny-Wundy ran like a flash to the other side of the creek, but he was so eager to get there, that he forgot to bring his tomahawk, which he had carelessly left on a boulder.

When the giant arose from the water, he looked around once again for Skunny-Wundy and did not see him, but he spotted the tomahawk. "What is this? It must be a toy!"

He picked up the tomahawk , and to test the sharpness of the blade, he put the blade to his tongue. "ARRGH!" he yelled, for the tomahawk was very sharp. The stone giant then used it to hit a rock and was very much surprised that the rock split in two.

Skunny-Wundy watched the stone giant. He had heard that the spit of a stone giant was magical, and he was now certain those words were true. Skunny-Wundy stepped boldly forward and began waving his arms about. "Now bring me my tomahawk and I will use it to cut off your head!"

The giant was now filled with fear since he had seen the tomahawk break a boulder in two. Now his stone skin would be no protection at all from the warrior who wielded it.

For the first time, the stone giant found himself begging for mercy. "No!" cried the giant. "It is true, Skunny-Wundy, you are a great warrior. Let me go, and I promise no stone giant will come near your village again."

Skunny-Wundy stood on the creek edge and pretended to contemplate this. He then nodded his head in agreement. "Yes," he said. "Go, run and save your life, but always remember what a great warrior I am."

The giant ran off into the woods leaving the now magical tomahawk on the bank of the creek. Skunny-Wundy waded over and retrieved his weapon. He returned to the village to tell the tale of how he used his wits, not his strength, to defeat the terrible stone giant.

The Stone Giant's Wife

Long ago, when a man went hunting, he would bring his wife with him. When he shot game, she would carry the game back and prepare it while the hunter remained in the woods and continued to hunt. One day in the woods, a hunter killed so much game that he and his wife needed to build a wigwam in which to store their kill. The hunter went off in one direction while his wife went in the opposite direction to fetch the game her husband had shot the prior day. As the wife returned to the wigwam with her game, she was startled to hear the sound of a woman singing. The lovely song floated out of the wigwam. However, to her horror, she found a stone giantess inside the wigwam nursing the wife's child.

"Don't fear," said the giantess. "I have run away from my cruel husband. I won't hurt you. I have come from far away, where the stone giants dwell, and I am very tired. I wish to stay with you and your husband a while, but you must cook my meat well, very long over the fire, for if I taste blood, I will want to kill you, your husband and your child."

The stone giantess said she would get the game the woman's husband had shot. The woman agreed and told her its location. Soon the stone giantess returned with a load so large it would have taken four men to have lifted. The woman then cooked their meal for them.

When the hunter returned, he was pleased to learn of the help the giantess had given his wife. The next day, however, after the hunter left, the stone giantess said, "My husband is cruel and brutal, and he is after me. In three days, he will be here. You and your husband must help me kill him when he comes. Don't worry, I will tell you what to do. I will tell you just where to strike him so you will pierce his wicked heart."

After the second day, she told the hunter he must stay home because her husband was coming. When the giant approached, she stood in the door, and as he grew near, she threw him down. The hunter and his wife ran toward him. "Strike him on the back!" the giantess yelled. "Now the neck!" The hunter deftly delivered the blows, and the stone giant was killed. The giantess dragged his body nearby and buried him, finally free of the oppressive creature.

The giantess stayed for a time with the hunter and his wife, making herself useful by cooking and carrying game. One day, she told them she must return home to her own people, for now she had no one to fear.

Burial of the Stone Giants at Onondaga

It is said the Tuscaroras were so tormented by the stone giants that they were forced to live in forts. They would select a piece of high ground, an overhang or a cliff, and then they would dig a trench and set upright timbers in it, one against the other, so that they stood several feet high. There were two entrances to the fort. One was for water, and the other was used as a sally port, according to Elias Johnson's book, *Legends, Traditions and Laws, of the Iroquois, or Six Nations*.

The stone giants continued to plague the Tuscaroras, and the situation grew increasingly grim. At last, the "Holder of the Heavens" visited his people on earth and decided something must be done to remedy the horrible situation. He transformed into a stone giant, took up a fearsome war club and joined them. The stone giants traveled on an expedition to find and torment the other five nations, an activity regularly enjoyed by the stone giants. By the time the giants approached the fort at Onondaga, they were tired from their journey. Their leader, the Holder of the Heavens, was artfully disguised as a stone giant, and he bade them to lie down near a mountain to rest, as

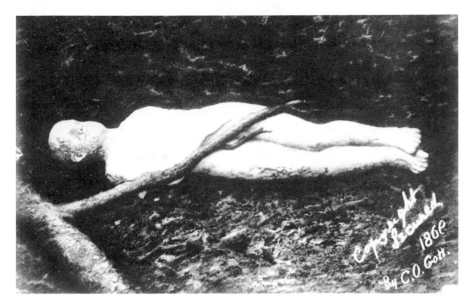

The Cardiff Giant. *Courtesy of the Library of Congress.*

the traditional time of attack was at first light. During the night, as the stone giants lay sleeping, the Holder of the Heavens ascended the mountain and sent down an avalanche of rocks, permanently burying the stone giants and bringing peace and tranquility to the Iroquois thereafter.

This story is why some believed that the Cardiff Giant found in nearby Cardiff was evidence of the legendary stone giants of the Iroquois.

BIGFOOT

There have been a number of Bigfoot sightings across New York State, including sightings in Central New York. Some claim the sightings go back all the way to the days before Europeans came to the New World. A few believe that the legend of the stone giants is a predecessor to the tales we tell about the wild man we call Bigfoot or Sasquatch today. Though occasionally sighted, precious few have been able to photograph or film Bigfoot. No bones belonging to the creature have ever been discovered, although some claim to have found footprints or other evidence, such as broken branches where it stood or walked in the woods.

There are enough current sightings to spark the imagination and make a hiker wonder if he should be on the lookout. In fact, recorded sightings of Bigfoot in New York State (excluding Iroquois stories of the stone giants) date back as early as 1818, up near Canada. The most notable early sighting was in 1869. Though still a bit outside of the Central New York region, this sighting was remarkable because the creature was seen running through the area shrieking loudly by about one hundred witnesses. This sighting occurred around Woodhill and Troupsville in Steuben County. The creature reportedly sported a long beard and horrible, long matted hair. Its eyes were bulging and bloodshot, and no one could tell if it was a man or a beast. More recent sightings described the creature as being more apelike than humanoid.

In 1899, there was a sighting in Dresden, New York, and the incident was reported in Central New York in the *Oswego Daily Times*. This description was of a dark-furred gorilla that was, oddly enough, wearing a red shirt (as we all know gorillas are want to do). This and the 1869 sighting could be reports of badly groomed, hirsute individuals—folks who might have taken advantage of electrolysis or laser hair removal had they lived at a later time. Still, reports continued to come in from Steuben County.

Locally, there have been recent sightings of Bigfoot listed in Oneida County and Herkimer County and more frequent ones in Chittenango of Madison County. Modern reports often describe a creature of great height, ranging from seven to nine and a half feet tall (nine feet is what is reported most often), and many estimate his weight to be between three and four hundred pounds. Most modern descriptions tell of a gorilla-like creature covered in dark hair, though some reports describe a more ruddy-colored Bigfoot. Often the creature is said to have extremely long arms, and at least one person has described Bigfoot as having hands. Witnesses have often experienced a feeling of being watched in the wilderness, and some claim that they saw Bigfoot either standing, kneeling or hunched over. People have also stated that they have heard sticks cracking and sometimes howling. Many times, the creature has run away, the witnesses have run in terror or both, so startled are they at the encounter. The beast has usually been seen in wooded areas or near the woods in clearings. A few have reported spotting Bigfoot along deserted roadsides. There have also been reports of the creature stealing chickens.

THE FLYING HEADS

There is a name for a horrifying creature that often tormented the Tuscaroras: Ko-nea-ra-yah-neh, otherwise known as the flying heads. Just the name "flying heads" brings to the imagination something that, by the laws of logic, should not even exist. Yet lore tells us they not only existed but also seemed to have thrived, tormenting and horrifying hapless Iroquois on a regular basis.

The heads themselves were large and humanoid, much larger than the size of a man's head. They were covered in hair and had long, flowing beards that flamed like fire, and they had the advantage of speed as well. They could fly through the air as fast as a shooting star. The result was that nobody could ever feel safe from an instant invasion.

A mere man could not protect himself from the horrific flying heads, for they possessed supernatural powers. The shamans declared the flying heads were a form of flowing power, and the people had no choice but to leave it to the shamans to defend them from the heads and remove the creatures with their magic. Even the most powerful and skillful warriors could not ward off the flying heads; rather, enchantments with drum and rattle were thought to be the only solution to the horrible situation. And yet, even these did not seem to rid the community of the monsters.

One day, a flying head came whirring though the air into the village. It lighted outside a particular lodge where only a single woman and her lone dog resided. The head perched itself just outside the window and peered inside greedily as it watched the woman, seated peacefully in front of the fire, carefully roasting acorns. Perhaps she did not notice the flying head as it watched her from behind, or perhaps her composure was so great that she could withstand its strange stare as it watched her go about her chore. The woman would take her acorns, place them in the fire and tend to them as they roasted. When they were ready, she carefully would remove each one from the fire and place them in her mouth to eat.

The flying head was filled with amazement, reverence and terror simultaneously. It stuck its tiny little paws out from beneath its great beard and hesitated momentarily, stunned by what it saw. It appeared this woman was sitting quietly in front of her fire, eating hot coals. A shiver of terror ran through the flying head, and he turned, quickly flying away, never to return. After that time, the flying heads ceased to torment the villagers and were never seen again.

LAKE MONSTERS

Fortunately for us here in Central New York, we have minimal exposure to lake monsters since most of the monster-filled lakes are exclusively in the Finger Lakes Region, but we do border Cayuga Lake and Lake Ontario, so it would be impossible to avoid a discussion about "Old Greeny," and the legendary monster of Lake Ontario. There is also, of course, the resident monster of Lake Owasco, located in Cayuga County. And who can forget the great man-serpent of the Iroquois?

The Monster of Lake Ontario

According to the Tuscarora tradition, after the creation of the world on the great Turtle's back, a horrific horned monster arose in the waters of Lake Ontario. Its breath was pure poison, and it caused many to become diseased. Numerous Indians died from their encounters with the monster. When the people could take these horrors no longer, the old women gathered and burned sacred tobacco and prayed to the Great Spirit. They asked that the Great Spirit send their great-grandfather, Thunder, to Earth to aid the people. Thunder, indeed, did come to the rescue of his people, and using his thunderbolts as his divine weapons, he chased the horned monster away into the deepest recesses of Lake Ontario. It may be there still.

The Enormous Serpent of the Iroquois

Though the Iroquois had periods where they lived peacefully, untroubled by supernatural monsters, there was a point where a great serpent with a human head arose and began to torment the Onondagas and Cayugas. The terrifying creature regularly parked itself on the very path that connected the Onondaga and the Cayuga nations, preventing anyone from passing. Long before there were paved roads across present-day New York State, there was an Iroquois footpath that connected all five nations of the Iroquois Confederacy. The man-serpent's obstruction of the road that connected the five nations cut the eastern nations off from the western nations. Communication and transport between the east and west became difficult and could not be accomplished in the normal way. At last, the nations coordinated a major attack on the great serpent, advancing on him simultaneously from all sides and attacking it with spears, arrows and darts. The battle was ferocious and much blood was shed. Eventually, the strange and horrible serpent was pierced and mortally wounded.

A sense of relief fell upon the Iroquois, and the death of the monster was celebrated by the people in both song and dance.

The Monster of Lake Owasco

No one can say if a monster has resided in Owasco Lake for centuries, but one was reported to exist by the *Post Standard* in its July 8, 1889 edition. The monster had been spotted by two fishermen on July 7. The two men, Fred C. Hayden and James O. Thomas, were fishing at Buck Point in the afternoon when they observed "a long, dark object" nearby in the water. At first, they attributed its motion to that of the water and imagined the object might have been an old stump. To get a better look at it, they stood in their trolling boat and saw the monster dive deep into the water. Both Thomas and Hayden were thought to be reliable witnesses of sound mind.

In mid-May 1897, a local farmer sighted the monster on the lake's eastern side in the morning. Soon after, two other witnesses saw what may have been the same creature floating on the top of the water, perhaps sunning itself. It was near Cascade and Indian Cove. The creature, however, rapidly swam away as they approached it.

Yet another report has surfaced from the *Auburn Daily Advertiser* on May 28, 1897. In this instance, two different unnamed fishermen described a shape they had seen in the water. It was astonishingly fifty feet long and three or four feet wide. The men drew closer in their boat out of curiosity and nearly sank as the center of the dark object began splashing wildly, creating waves that upset their craft.

At one point, a bounty of $100 was offered for the creature, but the creature was never captured, and the reward remained unclaimed.

"Old Greeny": the Monster of Cayuga Lake

"Old Greeny" has made numerous appearances over the years, as was reported by the *Ithaca Journal* on January 5, 1897. According to the paper, Old Greeny had been seen sixty-nine times. On that particular date, the monster had been seen by a resident of Ithaca and his friend on the eastern shore, and the creature was noted as quite large and serpentine.

Now and again, there were sightings of Old Greeny. Then, remarkably around 1929, the monster was seen with another of its kind on the eastern shore of Lake Cayuga. It was believed the creature was between twelve and fifteen feet in length.

Back then, some people theorized these were monsters that had infested the lake by traveling through yet undiscovered aquatic tunnels from Seneca

Lake, which was known to have similar serpents. Later, though, as modern underwater technology became more accessible, such underwater tunnels were not found, and that theory of origin was abandoned.

THE RO-TAY-YO OR GIANT MOSQUITO

Deep in your heart, you know giant mosquitoes exist. Central New York gets so much precipitation that mosquitoes can be a problem, but the Iroquois had it far worse, for they were plagued by a monster mosquito called the Ro-tay-yo, also known as the Ge-ne-un-dah-sais-ke. Enormous wings carried the insect, and it flew from place to place with its deadly, sword-like stinger, making a loud buzzing noise. We can only imagine the terror that sound must have struck into the hearts of men and women as they walked near lakeshores or stream banks. The Ro-tay-yo would land on a person and pierce his flesh with its mighty proboscis and then proceed to suck out every last ounce of his blood, leaving a lifeless body and no living witness behind. It was a creature both feared and loathed by all.

The Tuscaroras were the first tribe to encounter this loathsome insect along the Neuse River while their people still dwelled in what is today North Carolina. The Tuscaroras tried uselessly to defend themselves against the mighty mosquito but to no avail. Many warriors were killed, and the Ro-tay-yo thrived. Eventually, however, it flew off of its own accord, giving relief to the beleaguered tribe.

But once it had tasted the blood of Iroquoian victims, it lusted for more. Soon after vanishing from the Tuscaroras' North Carolina home, the Ro-tay-yo appeared near the fort at Onondaga and resumed its obnoxious attacks, buzzing the Onondagas and poking them with its stinger. Many died there also.

Tarenyawagon, a stately man with long, flowing hair who was known as the great benefactor of the Tuscaroras, made a visit to the fort to see the Onondaga chief. Just as he was arriving, the great mosquito buzzed by overhead. Tarenyawagon immediately sprang into action, trying to make an attack on the vexing creature, but its speed was so great that he could barely follow its flight with his eyes. Tarenyawagon began to pursue the mosquito toward the Great Lakes. He ran after the mosquito, crossing many miles of land as the sun was setting in the distance. He pursued the mosquito toward the east, then toward the west, not letting it have a moment of peace. At last, he was able to reach it, the creature having slowed a bit, perhaps out of exhaustion.

The mighty Tarenyawagon took his strong bow and aimed his arrow at the very heart of the Ro-tay-yo, killing it dead near the salt lake of Onondaga, called Gen-an-do-a. The great mosquito died, and its blood spilled forth. From its blood sprang the smaller species of modern mosquitoes that plague us even today.

THE GIANT MOSQUITO OF THE ONEIDAS

The different tribes of the Iroquois Confederacy often tell unique versions of tales. Fort Stanwix park ranger Susan Jones, who is of Native American descent (though not of Iroquois ancestry), told this Oneida Indian version of the Giant Mosquito myth.

Fort Stanwix, now a modern re-creation of a historic fort that stood on that same location, sat on a glacial formation. When the glacier melted, it formed an immense swamp that divided the Iroquois people. That swamp was guarded by a monster that had huge wings and a giant pointed stinger. The monster was, in fact, a giant mosquito, and it would think nothing of attacking any and all who dared venture near the swamp.

Stryker House on the site of Fort Stanwix. From Benson Lossing's *Pictoral Field Book of the Revolution. Courtesy of the Library of Congress.*

There was an Oneida brave who hoped to unite the Iroquois people once again. One day, he went forth into the great swamp armed only with a bow and arrow. He stalked the monster and shot his arrow straight through the heart of the mosquito, and it fell dead into the swamp. At first, all seemed well as he watched the monster die, but thousands of little insects—tiny mosquitoes—arose from its horrible corpse. Even today, if people come near a swampy area, they are attacked by those familiar tiny little monsters.

This story, Ranger Jones explained, teaches a number of lessons. It shows that there are times when one must take up arms to defend your people or perhaps family. It shows that it is important to do the right thing and that there are times when a warrior's bravery will be tested.

THE IROQUOIS LITTLE PEOPLE

Stories exist among the Iroquois of leprechaun-like beings known as Little People. While it might be difficult to imagine an Iroquois warrior shocked into a state of terror by a tiny man, many Iroquois traditionally feared the Little People. Some say that seeing one of the Little People is a bad omen. Others suggest just speaking of them will induce bad luck, yet stories and sightings of the Little People abound. The Little People are said to be easily offended, and though small in stature, their power is great. They demand respect. An offering of tobacco, however, often appeases the Little People, though the tiny folk can also be pleased by other forms of tribute, such as described in the following story, "Dirty Clothes and the Gifts of the Little People." They also offer great rewards to the givers as well. In addition to being diminutive, the Little People are considered magical. It is also important to note that Little People do not strictly appear to the Iroquois but to numerous Native American tribes. (Interestingly, the Irish also believe in Little People, or fairies. They believe that speaking of them could bring bad luck, and often fairies are called by a euphemism, such as "The Good People.") This section, however, will focus on the Iroquois Little People and the nonnative American Little People indigenous to Central New York.

Reportedly, the Little People were sighted in the past more often than they are today, which might be due to the fact that the modern Iroquois man seldom hunts for his food, nor is he found prowling the forests daily. Little People, after all, prefer secluded environments in nature. Nonetheless, I have met a Mohawk man who did see one. It was behind the structures on the Mohawk land in the community of Kanatsiohareke, west of Fonda near the

Mohawk River. One day, he saw a little man back there, dressed in buckskins like a traditional Iroquois, standing near the bushes. The Mohawk did not report to me that he encountered bad luck afterward but stressed that many believed speaking of the Little People was considered taboo. Silence was an act of self-protection. Nonetheless, stories of these mysterious people continue to circulate.

According to folklorist Arthur C. Parker, it is tradition to refrain from telling legends and tales during the warm season, as this is forbidden by the Little People; birds, bees and animals may become distracted by the tales, stopping to listen rather than concentrating on their work, such as building nests or making honey. According to Parker, the summertime storyteller may be reported to one of the chiefs of the Little People by a passing bird or another animal who spies what he is doing. All manner of misfortune may then befall the storyteller. Parker describes a few of the horrible possibilities, which include having your lips stung repeatedly by bees, having your tongue swell in your mouth or finding snakes occupying your bed that just might wrap themselves around your throat and suffocate you. So if you are considering telling these stories aloud during the summer, I heartily recommend you snap this book shut and mark it on your calendar to resume telling these tales after the first frost for your own personal safety. The Little People will not tolerate disobedience, so why take the risk? These stories will sound even more interesting in the winter as they would during the summertime, and you can read them completely unscathed.

Descriptions of the Little People tend to come from children having spotted them, as adults seem more likely to hear them or their water drums than to actually see them. However, of the descriptions that exist, we can say that they tend to be about a foot tall and are often dressed in a manner similar to that of the native Iroquois. Sometimes, however, they are seen cavorting about completely naked. It is said that they not only possess great strength but also have the ability to run very quickly. When the Iroquois heard the sound of the water drums, they knew that the Little People were holding a council meeting, and the Iroquois would then gather and make offerings to them to avoid their wrath. No one wished to become known for neglecting the Little People.

It is believed there are three tribes of Little People (or Pygmies, as they are sometimes called). One tribe makes its home along streams and under waterfalls. This tribe, known as the Stone Throwers, has great strength, and despite the people's tiny size, they are capable of uprooting trees by grabbing and twisting them with their tiny bare hands. They are also known for lifting and pitching sizable rocks or boulders—hence their name. The tossing of rocks isn't always random but rather a means to control the water level of rivers if the area is endangered by flooding. However, when not actively guarding the rivers, they have been known to perform recreational stone tossing, often luring Iroquois through their dreams for the purpose of holding a throwing competition or a type of Indian ball game. However, it would seem the competition is a bit one-sided, as the Stone Throwers are known for their ability to toss a rock skyward until it disappears entirely in the distance.

In times of drought, it was customary for the concerned Iroquois to go into the wild areas of the woods and seek out the streams, searching for evidence of the Stone Throwers. What these people were seeking were little hollow indentations of mud that are formed along the sides of the stream. These were significant and helpful in promoting rainfall. In case of drought, these would be carefully scooped up in a way that preserves their hollow structure. These little mud cups were then dried on a piece of bark. These cups are known as "dew cup charms," and for those who scoop them up, the cups should be placed in the lodge area to attract the Little People associated with fruits and grains who will bring abundant harvests to the garden. The Stone Throwers oversee the fish in the streams and rivers and have been known to release them from traps if they believe it is prudent. The Stone Throwers are easily offended, and when they were not remembered properly, they rewarded the offending Iroquois with drought and famine.

A second tribe concerns itself with the care of plants, fruits and vegetables. The tribe members oversee plants coming out of their winter dormancy, ensure the flowers bloom as they should and, just to be sure the fruit on the trees ripens properly, they carefully turn them so they get the proper solar exposure. As you might imagine, these Little People are loved and respected among the Iroquois for their dutiful labors amid the vegetable world. In the spring, these Little People begin their supernatural gardening activities with special emphasis on the strawberry plant, which is much celebrated among the Iroquois. Their work is a bit complicated and deserves some description. In the early spring, when frost still abounds, these helpful Little People help lessen the frost surrounding the beloved strawberry plants. They loosen the soil surrounding each plant so that it might grow easier. As needed, they turn each leaf carefully so that it can take advantage of the sun, which so often is in short supply in these parts. They readjust blossoms and plant the runners so that the strawberry plants might propagate. When delicious red fruits form, the helpful Little People do their best to protect the fruits from the ravages of insects. In particularly wet years, they also aid in the protection of the plants and fruits from the formation of mold. Once, in ancient times, the strawberry plant was stolen from the face of the earth and remained underground, hidden from mankind for many centuries. It was eventually returned to earth by a sunbeam, and now the plant gets special attention from both the Little People and humans alike. The Little People watch it with hawk-like vigilance, and the Iroquois hold special celebrations to give thanks for the great gift of the strawberry plant.

These Little People are intensely attuned to seeds and growing vegetation. It is their mission in life to assist the myriad of plant forms, from the smallest seedling to mature plants. They hide in dark places and listen to the sounds of the seedlings deep within the earth and cater to their needs. They add color to the plants and adjust them so that they receive the optimum amount of sunlight. They turn the fruits so that they ripen fully and have been known to turn leaves as well. It is because of this intense care and special labor that this tribe of Little People is so very well respected. Without their wisdom and vigilance, it would be difficult or impossible to farm or garden with any amount of success. Here in Central New York, surrounded by such vast quantities of green vegetation, it is difficult not to appreciate their endless labor.

This tribe of Little People sometimes takes different forms. In the course of the Little People's duties, they may appear to the Iroquois as a variety of birds or as bats, but their radically altered appearance bears meaning. Each form is assumed to convey a particular message to the people. For instance, when one of this tribe appears in the form of a robin, then the news he brings is good. However, if he appears in the form of an owl, then the people know they should be on the lookout for trouble that is afoot. The owl form is a warning to the knowledgeable Iroquois; if he sees an owl, then he knows that he should keep alert, for someone may be trying to deceive him. A bat warns of a struggle to the death. Each messenger should be heeded.

The third tribe makes its home in underground caverns and caves, and these Little People act as guards to the underworld. As a result, the members of this tribe are seldom seen by humans. Unlike what some might expect, there is a world inside the earth. There are great forests and plains, and these regions of the inner earth are filled with a vast variety of animal life, which the third tribe stands guard over. And guard they must, for the majority of creatures who dwell beneath the earth wish to come forth onto the face of the earth and dwell in the full light of day. They, therefore, frequently plot their escape into our world, the world of sunlight. This third tribe, then, is always on guard. They are good at their work, but from time to time, animals do break free. In those cases, these Little People must round them up and herd them below once again.

The Little People have the ability and capacity to make individuals ill, but they also have the capacity to help or cure. One must not offend them lest he or she suffer their wrath, but by the same token, if the Little People are pleased, they might well give you aid or special gifts or help. In addition to desiring the gift of tobacco, Little People also covet human fingernail clippings. These are gathered into little bags and left as offerings. The Little People are said to wet the bags and bathe with them so they can absorb the smell of mankind. That scent, as it turns out, is useful; when animals smell the human scent of the clippings on them, they often turn away from the Little People, leaving them unharmed or let the Little People approach and, consequently, have a better chance in their hunting. In this way, the bundles of nail clippings are thought quite desirable and make excellent gifts or offerings of appeasement.

In the following story, an Iroquois youth called Dirty Clothes encounters two Little People and decides to spend four days with them. However, upon returning to his village, he discovers many years have passed. The similarity between the tale of Dirty Clothes, Irish fairy lore and Washington Irving's "Rip Van Winkle" (which many believe was based on German folklore) is apparent. Stories of a man meeting with otherworldly beings, spending time with them and finding that great expanses of time have passed instead of just a short while have existed in various parts of the world, and this Iroquois story is yet another example of that.

Dirty Clothes and the Gifts of the Little People

Once, there was an orphan who lived with his uncle, but he was not treated well. In fact, his uncle made it a point to dress the boy in rags, so the people then gave him the name "Dirty Clothes."

Still, the boy was a good hunter and skillful with a bow and arrow. One day, he was walking near some cliffs that rose precipitously from the water where the Little People (also called Jo-Ge-Oh) were said to play their drums. The villagers feared the place, as many believed to see a Little Person was a bad omen and ill luck would come to whomever saw one. Dirty Clothes, however, remembered his dead mother's wise words. She had often told him to walk with good in his heart, and he would have nothing to fear. The boy headed those words. That day already, he had shot two squirrels, and they hung from his belt.

Dirty Clothes saw a hickory tree near the water, and his eyes followed a black squirrel jumping from branch to branch. Suddenly, he heard a voice yell, "Shoot again, my brother! Your arrow has missed the squirrel."

Dirty Clothes looked around to find the two men, and to his amazement, two tiny men with bows and arrows stood by his feet. He watched as the one took aim at the squirrel, but as before, his arrow fell short. Dirty Clothes knew the little man would never hit the squirrel like that, so he raised his bow and fired an arrow, hitting his mark. The black squirrel fell swiftly from the tree.

The two hunters ran quickly toward the squirrel and exclaimed, "Who shot this arrow?" Then, upon looking up, they saw the boy. "You shoot well," said the little man. "The squirrel is yours."

Dirty Clothes thanked them and said, "No, the squirrel is yours, as are the two on my belt as well."

The two little men were overjoyed. One said, "Come, we will take you to our lodge and you will enjoy our hospitality." Dirty Clothes gladly followed them to the river, but he was troubled when he saw a tiny canoe bobbing on the water, no bigger than a shoe. Dirty Clothes knew even his bare foot would sink such a small craft. He looked at the two little men who beckoned him to climb in. With trepidation, Dirty Clothes took a step into the canoe and instantly found himself as tiny as the two other sailors.

The two hunters then dipped their paddles into the cool water of the stream, but instead of sailing forward, the tiny craft moved skyward, rising above the hickory and the oak, toward the cliffs where the Little People resided.

Once inside, the two told their people how Dirty Clothes had killed the black squirrel. "Please stay with us for a short while, so that we might teach you," they implored.

Dirty Clothes stayed, and the Little People taught him many things about the birds and the animals of the forest. He learned about corn, beans and squash and how they could feed his people. They told him about strawberries, which could be plucked from the forest floor at the beginning of summer, and they showed him how to make a beverage that the Little People enjoyed. They also taught Dirty Clothes a special dance that he could perform in the dark so the Little People could join him, unseen, in the dance. By performing this dance in a darkened place, he could thank the Little People for their many gifts.

Dirty Clothes stayed for four days among the Little People, but he knew that he should head home soon and return to his own village and his people. The two little men he had met while hunting in the woods then walked him toward his home, stopping many times to teach him about various plants and animals. He studied each living thing they showed him and learned their names.

When Dirty Clothes reached a spot near the edge of his village, he turned to speak to his friends, only to discover that he was standing alone in a field. He marveled at how much these people had taught him in only four days' time.

As he walked into the village, he also noticed how much his own village had changed in just four days. Clearly, it was his village, but it was different, too.

At last a woman approached him and announced, "Stranger, you are welcome here, but please tell us who you are."

Dirty Clothes was stunned. "Don't you recognize me? I am Dirty Clothes."

"How is that possible?" replied the woman. "Look at you! See how fine your clothes are?"

Dirty Clothes looked down at himself for the first time. He was no longer dressed in dirty torn rags. Instead, he wore a fine buckskin that was embroidered with the hair of the moose and with porcupine quills.

He asked the woman where his uncle was, pointing to his old lodge. "Oh," said the woman, "Why would a man like you look for someone the likes of him?" Dirty Clothes told the woman that man was his uncle, and the woman explained that he had died long ago.

Once again, Dirty Clothes looked at himself and realized that he was no longer a boy but a strong young man dressed in fine buckskin. He was taller now than many in his village. It was then that Dirty Clothes realized how much the generous Little People had really given him, and Dirty Clothes began to tell his story.

All the people listened to Dirty Clothes's tale, and he explained to them the many things he had learned while he was with them. That night, he taught them the Dark Dance, and the people performed it for the first time. As they danced, they were joined by unseen people, who sang with them, happy to hear their gratitude.

The Little People still come in friendship when the people of the long house perform the Dark Dance, even to this very day.

The Dark Dance

The Dark Dance Ceremony was described by Parker, a Seneca Indian. The ceremony was very likely similar to that practiced by the Central New York Iroquois tribes. While the story above makes it sound as if there is only 1 song for the Dark Dance ritual, Parker claims that it consists of 102 songs and is divided into four distinct sections, all of which are sung in the dark. Edmund

Wilson described the ceremony as consisting of 168 songs, however, and he specifies that a song is similar to a stanza in a ballad with nonsense words in the refrain.

There are four sections to the Dark Dance. During the ceremony, the Little People might join in the singing, and it is said that sometimes their voices are heard but not understood, as they sing in a foreign tongue. When the Little People enter during the song, there is a great shuffling of feet as the little ones trip and maneuver around everyone's feet in the dark. It seems to some a bit frightening. During the ceremony, the water drum and horn rattle are played. Singers, musicians and observers might sit tight against the wall so dancers may have space on the floor. Since the Dark Dance is performed in homes rather than in a long house, space is tighter. Custom dictates that someone hosts the feast, and people eat between the segments of the dance. During those times, the lights are turned back on.

As the Little People are easily offended, the ceremony acts as a means to appease them and can also be used to ask for their aid. During the ceremony, an invocation is given and tobacco is burned as an offering to the Little People.

Non-Iroquois Little People

Native Americans were not the only groups to report sightings of Little People in this region. Aaron S. Popple told me a story of a sighting he made as a boy growing up in a small village located in Madison County.

I was about five or so. We moved with my stepdad to his country farm. Whitelaw, New York was, and still is, sparsely populated. It was December, just before Christmas of 1978. There was snow on the ground. The moon was almost full. If any of you have ever lived in the Snowbelt, you will know the type of night this was, with crisp air, clear skies, a full moon and snow on the ground. It was very bright outside on that night. I was sitting looking out the west window towards the road. There were no cars out that late in those days. I was looking for shooting stars, and it was too cold to be outside, so instead I looked out my window. Then three Little People came out of nowhere. They were running down the road when they noticed me in the window. One pointed. They waved, and they then did acrobatics in the road!!! I could see their silhouettes, pointy jester hats and shoes with the toes curled up. They were all doing somersaults, and one was juggling. They waved good-bye and took off down the road on their way!!!

Left: Whitelaw Church. Whitelaw is a small community where the Little People are said to have flourished for generations. *Photo courtesy of the author.*

Below: A sign and field of flowers in Whitelaw. A beautiful natural setting is the perfect environment for a colony of Little People. *Photo courtesy of the author.*

I immediately woke my mom up to tell her that Santa's elves had just been there to check up on me! Of course, this was met with the usual parental response. It took me a while to not believe in Santa. I saw his freaking elves! Over the years, I have written this off as unexplained, or maybe I dozed off and had a dream. After all, it was rather late at night.

But just tonight, I was visiting with my tenant who grew up in this area, and he claims that he was riding with his boss, a local farmer from up the road. Then, out of blue, two Little People ran out in front of them as they drove by our farmhouse. The elves were dressed in wool coats and pointy shoes. This guy is four years older than me, and he was sixteen at the time. He then told me of another farmer who always said "the Little People are here in Whitelaw."

People have allegedly seen little folk skating on a pond in Whitelaw too. Ten years ago a neighbor girl told me she used to camp out in her tree house. She claims to have heard little scampering noises, giggling and weird music playing in the forest floor below.

MUMMIES OF CENTRAL NEW YORK

Mummies usually originate from desert cultures, from places so dry that human and animal flesh will desiccate without intervention, naturally preserving a body after death. It is only a small leap, then, for such cultures to create a system of mummification to preserve a body for the journey into the afterlife. It is hard to imagine mummies originating in a place as damp as Central New York, and in fact, they did not. Certainly, however, there were a number of mummies imported from Egypt into this region. This section tells the story of one of those, a mummy named "Hen," and the strange case of newspapers made out of mummy wrappings.

Hen, the Egyptian Mummy

If you travel to the Cazenovia Library, a stately Greek Revival building located on Route 20, you will find a rare treat tucked away inside the library's museum: a two-thousand-year-old Egyptian mummy named Hen. The mummy is now estimated to be a male, approximately twenty-five years old, but it was originally believed to be a middle-aged woman.

The mummy is called "Hen" due to the three-letter word inscribed on the sarcophagus cover: "May the King and Osiris, Chief of the West [the land of the dead], the great god, lord of Abydos, be pleased to give a

Cazenovia Public Library houses an unusual display of ancient artifacts. *Photo courtesy of the author*.

The top of Hen's sarcophagus. *Photo courtesy of the author*.

The top of Hen's sarcophagus. *Photo courtesy of the author.*

View of Hen, the Egyptian mummy. *Photo courtesy of the author.*

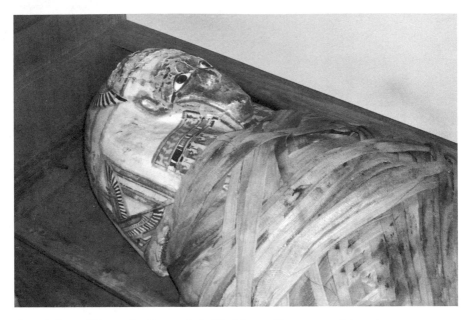

Frontal view of Hen at the Cazenovia Public Library. *Photo courtesy of the author.*

mortuary offering of bread, beer, oxen and fowl [for] the one beloved of the great god: Hen." At least it can be said that "Hen" is most likely part of the mummy's name, as the final portion of the inscription appears missing.

Male or female, young or old, it seems unlikely that one would find an ancient Egyptian mummy in a small village in Central New York. The story of this mummy's arrival began when Robert James Hubbard, a wealthy Cazenovia businessman, purchased John William's 1830 Greek Revival home in 1890. He planned to use it to house Cazenovia's new library. The original library, which consisted of approximately two hundred volumes, had been located in John William's general store on Albany Street (off Route 20), which was not far away. But the building was not Hubbard's final gift to the community. In the 1890s, there was much excitement about the remarkable treasures of Egypt. Hubbard was determined to take a Grand Tour with his son, Robert, to Egypt, Europe and the Middle East and purchase a mummy or two, as well as an assortment of Egyptian and other antiquities for a new museum that would open on the second floor of the library. Today, Robert Hubbard's diary of this remarkable journey is housed at the Lorenzo State Historic Site in Cazenovia, and his diary tells the story of that extraordinary ten-month journey.

Hubbard and his son departed from Cazenovia on December 30, 1893, and traveled to New York City. The two later sailed from Sandy Hook, New Jersey. They encountered rough seas for much of their journey. In fact, the storms were so violent that a ship that sailed three days behind them was forced to return to New York due to immense tidal waves. Though the ship was undoubtedly luxurious, the journey was uncomfortable; many of those on board experienced motion sickness, and Hubbard ate little during the voyage. However, on January 22, they arrived on the Island of Pico

Robert Hubbard. *Photo used with permission of the Cazenovia Public Library. Photo courtesy of the author.*

where they changed ships to embark on *The Spree*, arriving at Gibraltar on January 25. The two did some sightseeing in Genoa, Italy, before continuing their journey. They arrived in Naples on January 31, and with glee, Hubbard and his son spent the day visiting Pompeii. They then viewed Mount Etna and finally arrived at Port Said in Egypt on Sunday, February 4, 1894 after nineteen days of travel. They could see the muddy effect of the great Nile far out to sea, as well as the numerous English and German vessels docked there. The following day, Hubbard and his son took a train to Cairo, finally arriving on February 5.

Upon his arrival, Hubbard's expectations of Cairo were shattered as he was greeted by various celebrations of Carnival, what he described as "foolishness introduced by the English." The population participating in the excitement surely could not grasp its meaning. The streets below the hotel were decorated in vivid colors and filled with all manner of people from various countries. Hubbard had brought sweets from home, and they tossed the candy and confetti into the crowd as the procession passed, and the people eagerly jumped to receive the treats. They were unable to do anything else that day, presumably because of the celebrations.

What impressed Hubbard about Cairo were the innovations such as the train. He noted the irrigation canals and the devices that helped bring water to the wheat crops, which supported the sizable population. He also noted that many still lived in one-story abodes, much in the same manner as Egyptians did in biblical times.

While in Cairo, Hubbard and his son lived in style, staying at the prestigious Shephard's Hotel. They visited a historic mosque and the tombs of the Caliphs and drove through the picturesque streets of Cairo, visiting various shops. Hubbard noted in his journal, "[The merchandise was] very attractive, but we restricted all importunities to buy—simply examining."

On February 8, Hubbard and his son drove to the Museum of Boulaq and visited its treasures. (This museum was originally in Boulaq, but was moved to Giza after a flood damaged the museum's structure in 1878. Since 1902 it has been located in Cairo and is now known as The Museum of Egyptian Antiquities.) They visited the pyramids, and Hubbard hired donkey boys and attendants for the outing. He also hired, at great expense, a man to keep away people who were attempting to solicit the party. But, Hubbard notes, "He only played into their hands." Apparently, the donkey boys annoyed them constantly as well. There were high winds, and the blowing sand made it uncomfortable for the party as they made their way first to the sphinx and then to the excavated temple. People were hired to push and pull them to the top of the pyramid and back down its slippery surface. "I wouldn't do it again," Hubbard wrote in his diary. "It was dirty and fatiguing once done [and] will not be repeated."

Over the next few days, they witnessed whirling dervishes and a horse fair. They visited the bazaar, watched the sun set behind the pyramids and even visited Jacob's Well and the levee on the Nile.

Then, on Sunday, February 11, 1894, after Hubbard and his son had attended the English Church and lunched at the Palace Hotel, they returned to visit the museum in the afternoon. They went into the sales room, where duplicates are disposed of at apparently very moderate prices. A mummy and case can be had for £20 or £30, and scarabs sold between 5 pence and 20 pence a piece. The mummy "Hen" was purchased for £20, and would be valued at nearly $2,000 in today's money.

While in Egypt, Hubbard purchased a wide variety of specimens including a mummified cat and an ibis. The collection he amassed for the library included mortuary lamps (thought it's unclear if Hubbard purchased one or many), a scarab beetle and shabtis (pronounced *shawb*-tee), which are small clay figurines that are meant to be buried with the mummy so that they may

A cat mummy on display at the Cazenovia Public Library. *Photo courtesy of the author.*

Page, the library cat, eyes the taxidermic birds. *Photo courtesy of the author.*

be called upon to perform whatever labor was required by the dead person during his or her afterlife. These objects and others, including examples of mummy wrappings, were obtained in Egypt. Other objects were purchased or collected on the remainder of Hubbard's tour through the Middle East and Europe.

After obtaining these Egyptian artifacts, Hubbard had them shipped back to Cazenovia in 1894, though he and his son did not return until 1895.

When they did return, his collection was unpacked and a grand display was assembled on the second floor of the library. To introduce the mummy to the people of Cazenovia and to raise funds for the new library, a "Mummy Tea" was held. Here is a description of the event that was published in 1895 in the *Cazenovia Republican*:

> *The mummy rests in the bottom of a new glass case in one of the upper rooms of the house, and to the disappointment of many people, is not entirely unwrapped. It seems that after the embalming process was finished, a hollow mask of substance resembling paper mache, and large enough to cover the head and shoulders of the deceased, was slipped into position, and below this narrow strips of cloth were wound around the body and back over the mask itself. The windings were then covered with other windings of wider cloth, until the body became quite bulky, when it was placed in its coffin and laid away. In this case, all the wrappings except the first layer had been removed, exposing the mask, but not the face. The face of the mask was gilded, and the gilding and painting is as fresh after 2000 years, as it was when first put on.*
>
> *The strips of cloth with which it is wound are yellow with age, and are wound in exactly the same pattern as the familiar log cabin bed quilt—another illustration that there is nothing new under the sun.*
>
> *The reason for retaining some of the coverings to the mummy was explained by the appearance of a skull on another shelf—all that remained of another mummy unrolled in Mr. Hubbard's presence last year, the other parts of the body having crumbled on exposure to air.*
>
> *On the topmost shelf of the cabinets reposes the wooden coffin in which the body had been entombed, showing no decay, the marks of the saw and plane still visible and showing the curious way of fastening it together with small wooden pins instead of nails. On the other shelves are arranged many other funerary curios of the ancient Egyptians such as the small image of Osiris the great god and king of the underworld, covered with hieroglyphics, mummy necklaces of rude beads, tear bottle, mummified ibis, and cat, images of Ra, the eagle headed god, scarabs, etc.*

Originally, the Cazenovia mummy was thought to be a woman. Between 1944 and 1945, the hieroglyphics were translated on the sarcophagus by the Metropolitan Museum of Art in New York City from photographs, and the mummy's partial name, Hen, was discovered. However, no sophisticated medical analysis was available at the time, and the mummy was dated to the late Greco-Roman period, somewhere between AD 332 and 395, as determined by the diamond pattern wrapping method of the mummy (although the coffin was thought to be from the later, Ptolemaic period). The dating was also determined from photographs sent by the curator to New York. Though this mummy has his hands neatly folded across his chest, an indication of royalty in the Greco-Roman era, this death pose was later commonly used by people of a variety of statuses.

The first medical analysis of the mummy was conducted in 1984, when it was transported to the Oneida City Hospital for X-ray. The mummy was petite in size, measuring only five feet four inches, and because of that and the shape of its pelvis, it was presumed the mummy was likely a woman,

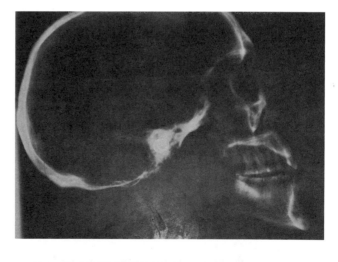

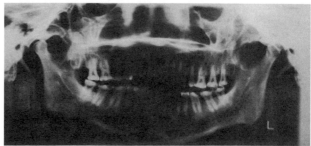

X-rays of the mummy's skull. *Photo courtesy of the author.*

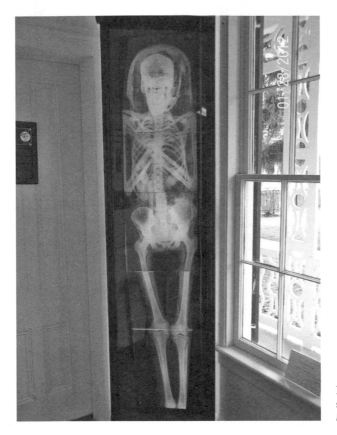

X-ray of the mummy's skeleton. *Photo courtesy of the author.*

somewhere between thirty and fifty years old. No artifacts were found on the mummy through X-ray, although Harris growth arrest lines were shown on the skeleton, indicating the mummy had experienced trauma or illness during growth. The cause of death could not be determined.

The mummy was examined again in 1994. The curator was concerned that the mummy may have experienced deterioration due its age and the lack of temperature and humidity control in the 1830 Cazenovia Library building. A mobile X-ray unit was then employed, and it used low kilovoltage nonscreen radiography to examine the mummy.

A further analysis of the mummy was performed by Dr. E. Mark Levinsohn, a medical doctor at Crouse Radiology Associates in Syracuse. This analysis used different techniques and yielded new and, in some instances, opposite results from the previous studies.

To determine a more specific and accurate age, samples of the mummy wrapping were taken from the foot area and were carbon dated and tested by chemical analysis. The wrapping was composed of flax, the plant fiber used to make linen, and it was carbon dated to 104 BCE, give or take forty years. This has been taken as the new, more accurate date of death for the mummy Hen.

The medical examiner and staff from Crouse placed Hen on a stretcher, and the mummy was transported by ambulance to Crouse Hospital where it was subjected to CT scanning. Interestingly, the first scan, a full-body scan, yielded so much data that it overwhelmed their computers and the mummy had to be rescanned in segments. The scans revealed that Hen was in extremely good condition. Here are some of the results: as expected, no brain was found to be present in the mummy, as ancient Egyptians believed that organ to be rather insignificant. Other organs were routinely preserved and replaced in mummy bodies, but the brain had been carefully removed through the nasal cavities and discarded. The skull was complete, and the teeth showed little wear, which suggested the individual had a bread diet that was sand free (that is, made with good flour).

There was some flesh present, and this, along with other images, was used to recreate a probable face for the mummy Hen. The face shown was quite elongated and had large eyes and an elongated nose. The artist had bone, skin, ear and nose cartilage to help flesh out the two-thousand-year-old face of Hen.

One interesting feature they discovered was that the jaw was tied shut so that the mouth would remain closed. Though tying a jaw shut is common mortuary practice today, it is not frequently found among ancient Egyptian mummies.

Mummy Paper

Each day, here in Central New York (as well as the nation at large), we see newspapers shrinking and smaller newspaper publishers consolidating or vanishing as more people read the news online, if they read the news at all. However, this was not always the case for newspapers. In the 1850s, America's newspapers flourished, so much so that rag shortages occurred as the young nation struggled to supply its presses. The papers back then were composed of rag linen rather than tree pulp as they are today, and it was not uncommon for paper makers to collect recycled linens from homemakers and other sources. While this made newspapers durable, it also caused papers to vary in appearances as the sources of the linen varied. Even today, a tabloid newspaper that concentrates on scandals, gossip and seedy subject matter can be referred to as a "rag." Supplying these hungry presses became a problem. Each day, new supplies were required to print the news for an eager readership.

There was a particular paper mill located in Broadalbin, New York, that was rumored to use mummy wrappings for the rags processed to produce the daily paper. This story comes from a Mrs. John Ramsey of Syracuse who shared the tale of a family friend who had been employed by the mill and whose position required that he unwrap the mummies the mill received. Reportedly, the problem was that once the wrappings were unrolled, they would immediately bounce back into the shape of the mummy, having been in that form for perhaps some several thousand years. The mummy wrappings were extremely difficult to work with, but with the shortage of rags, there wasn't a viable alternative. Mrs. Ramsey's friend worked at the mill from 1855 to 1860. The wrappings were said to be of a cream color, some of them bearing embroidered work along the edges.

The rag shortage apparently began around 1854 and was caused by a shift in Italian rag exports to England instead of America, leaving hapless paper mills such as the Broadalbin one no recourse but to strip ancient rags off of desiccated corpses imported from Egypt.

While some might think the tale preposterous, the July 31, 1856 issue of the *Syracuse Standard* claimed to be printed on Egyptian rags that the Marcellus Falls plant had processed. The rags are said to have been imported by Mr. G.W. Ryan. Reportedly, there was a clear textural difference in the July 31, 1856 issue of the *Syracuse Standard*, and eager readers might yet have the opportunity to feel the edition located at the Onondaga Historical Association. Some claimed that the rags had been stripped from mummies, although the *Standard* did not go so far as to make that claim.

CHAPTER FOUR

CURIOUS PLACES IN CENTRAL NEW YORK

THE HOUSE OF JOSIAH WHIPPLE JENKINS

The village of Vernon is well known for its horse racing track, but the villagers have valued their horses for centuries. And while a horse is generally not considered a mysterious animal, this next story will be of interest to history buffs, for this remarkable horse spent his later years in a stable behind the house of Josiah Whipple Jenkins at 4 Ward Street. Captain James Jenkins of Vernon, New York, served in the Union army during the Civil War, fighting to eradicate slavery, a cause his family championed. In fact, James Jenkins was the son of Josiah Whipple Jenkins, the lawyer who defended John Brown. The Jenkins family was close to abolitionist Gerrit Smith's family as well. Captain Jenkins served at the Battle of Appomattox, and as it turned out, Jack, his horse, played a major role during the ceremony in which General Robert E. Lee surrendered to General Ulysses S. Grant.

Captain Jenkins was in charge of the Oneida Cavalry, which escorted commanding Union general George B. McClellan during the latter part of the Civil War. After Richmond was evacuated, Captain Jenkins was placed in command of forwarding ammunition, and the Oneida Cavalry was split. Some remained with Captain Jenkins; the rest were stationed at Union headquarters with Sergeant Stewart.

When the time came for the surrender, a saddle horse was sought for General Grant to ride, his own horse having gone lame. The order came to Sergeant Stewart from a man whose name was either Colonel Ingalls or Ingersoll. There were a number of horses available, but Jack was a fine sorrel,

Above: General Lee prepares to surrender to General Grant on April 9, 1895. *Courtesy of the Library of Congress.*

Left: General Grant and his warhorse, 1864. *Courtesy of the Library of Congress.*

fifteen hands high and chestnut-colored. He was, by all accounts, a handsome horse and held his head erect. He had a fine appreciation for martial music, and whenever he heard it, he proudly pranced, lifting his legs high like the finest show horse. It then came as no surprise that Jack was selected to carry the victorious General Grant to receive General Lee's surrender.

Jack originally belonged to a farmer and was taken by the government to be used in the war. The farmer was paid for Jack with a government voucher. After the war, Jack was given to Captain Jenkins after his horse had been killed in battle, and Captain Jenkins brought Jack home to Vernon. But Jack proved to be a lazy horse; very little could motivate him outside of his love of military music. He also feared loud noises and the clank of metal. It was said that if you touched him with a riding crop, he would run a few paces and then slow down to a trot, and the only way to make him run was to clank some metal together. Then and only then would the horse move at full speed.

After his retirement from the army, Old Jack was kept at the Jenkins home in Vernon and was ridden in the annual Declaration Day (known today as Memorial Day) procession, where he donned a colorful wreath of flowers around his beautiful brown neck. He made quite an appearance in the parade, as did his companion horse, Don.

Don was a bay horse with an impressive black tale and black mane. He had been given to David Jenkins, James's brother, by a man from Rome, New York, when Don was just three years old. Unlike Jack, Don was lively and active, and David rode the bay until David was killed at the Battle of the Wilderness at the age of twenty-eight. Don was then brought back home and spent the rest of his life in Vernon. Both horses lived to be over thirty years

Pencil drawing by Edwin Forbes entitled *Wounded Soldiers Crossing the Rappahannock River at Fredericksburg on a Flatboat—After the Battle of the Wilderness*. Courtesy of the Library of Congress.

Burial of Union soldiers at Fredericksburg, Virginia, May, 1864. *Courtesy of the Library of Congress.*

old and are buried in unmarked graves in the yard at the Jenkins' home. They were said to be buried in a pasture on a hill under some elm trees, but Dutch elm disease subsequently devastated the village's elm population and prevented anyone from locating the burial sites.

David Tuttle Jenkins bears a bit more attention. Though he lived a short life, he was very heroic. He was born in 1836, and when his father died in 1852, he became the support of the Jenkins family and the head of the household at the Jenkins home in Vernon. He had begun a course of study in the city of Troy at Rensselaer Polytechnic Institute, but his health began to fail him, and he was forced to abandon his pursuit of a degree in engineering. He later decided to study law and follow in his father's footsteps. The Civil War, however, disrupted his plans.

Since David was supporting his family, he was immune to the draft. His family needed him for its subsistence. Still, David felt the strong tug of patriotism and went about the task of raising three Oneida County regiments. By the summer of 1862, he was preparing to raise yet a fourth regiment, but he found it impossible to continue to ask others to risk their lives in battle without placing his on the line as well, and so he, too, joined the war. He served as the adjutant of the 146th Regiment, serving under Colonel Garrard. Before his unit was deployed, however, David Jenkins was promoted to major and then to lieutenant colonel. In time, he became colonel of his regiment.

David Jenkins fought at the battle of Little Round Top and was wounded there. He recovered and was again up for a promotion while fighting in the Battle of the Wilderness in May 1864. But during the fight, he went missing.

When news of his disappearance reached Vernon, Electra Jenkins, David's mother, and Everett Case, a family friend, immediately went south to scour the battlefield in search of David. Their efforts were, unfortunately, in vain, and David's body was never recovered. It had been a horrible and bloody battle, and the search must have been heart-wrenching, but Electra Jenkins persevered. The total number of casualties from the battle was so immense that it is no wonder Electra Jenkins was unable to locate the body of her son David. Union casualties for that battle were 2,246. In addition, 12,037 were wounded, and 3,383 were captured or missing. On the Confederate side, 1,495 were killed, 7,928 wounded and 1,702 captured or missing. The battle was considered inconclusive—neither a victory for the Union nor a defeat but devastating nonetheless. But Electra did learn that her son had behaved heroically on the first day of battle, supporting himself with his sword and a tree after taking two bullets, one to the head and another to the body. It was presumed David could not have survived these wounds.

THE SECRET ROOM BENEATH THE JENKINS HOUSE

Perched high on a hill overlooking the village of Vernon is a magnificent home currently occupied by Edith Monsour. It was built in 1844 by Josiah Whipple Jenkins and is now known as Woodlawn. Originally, Jenkins intended to have the house built in Greek Revival style, but midway into its construction, he changed his mind, favoring an Italianate style. The building is handsome to be sure, but what perhaps fascinates most about the structure is not what is seen but rather what is unseen.

Hidden beneath Woodlawn's sturdy walls is a secret room that is said to be a hiding spot used on the Underground Railroad. According to the

The Jenkins Home, now known as Woodlawn. *Photo courtesy of the author.*

story, there is a tunnel beneath the house that connected to a route that surreptitiously led to nearby Peterboro, known to be the place where abolitionist Gerrit Smith hid and transported slaves en route to Canada after the Fugitive Slave Law was passed in 1850. Before that time, if a slave made it north, even crossing the border from Virginia to Washington, D.C., he had obtained freedom. There would have been no need for a system in the north to hide and transport slaves to Canada until 1850. We can presume then that it would not have been necessary to install tunnels, secret rooms and phony cisterns for that purpose during the construction of the Jenkins home in 1844.

The fake cistern, located in the cellar at the opposite end of that grand house from the real cistern, is not made in the manner of the original construction. It appears to have been added after the house had already been built. Josiah Whipple Jenkins died of tuberculosis in 1852, only two years after the Fugitive Slave Law was passed. It is unknown whether it was he who had this structure installed or another family member later. Both sons and their mother, Electra Jenkins, were strong supporters of

Above: The false cistern in the Jenkins House basement below the stairs. *Photo courtesy of Francis Zimmer.*

Right: Looking southeast at the false cistern in the Jenkins House basement. *Photo courtesy of Francis Zimmer.*

the Union cause, but the author suspects it may have been Josiah Jenkins who installed this structure, as the economic circumstances of the family degraded considerably after his death.

Edith described two cisterns in the basement of her home. One is an actual cistern made to hold water. The second, however, is a false cistern that could act as a hiding place. Three rooms were said to be behind the cistern, and a tunnel that was believed to exit onto Peterboro Road. (According to the Vernon Historical Society, there was an Underground Railroad home with a tunnel located on Peterboro Road). The secret room has not seen much use in the last 150 years. At one point, Richard Monsour entered the false cistern. It was so filthy that he came out covered with debris. The alleged tunnel was said to run below the back hallway of the house, heading in an eastward direction and paralleling the Old Seneca Turnpike, now called Route 5. Three rooms containing junk, debris and old bones, which were suspected to be the remains of fugitives' meals, were believed to be along the length of the tunnel. Additionally, there is a six-foot drop to enter the cistern that requires a ladder to access, so it is clear that such a tunnel would not have been used by the family for convenience.

My husband and I were invited to descend into the false cistern and photograph it. We were not sure what we would find, but after hearing about the dirt involved, we wore our worst clothes and brought hard hats and paper masks to protect ourselves from dust and debris. Edith said we would be able to use her six-foot aluminum ladder to enter and exit the cistern.

The first thing we studied was the actual cistern for the house. The Jenkins home was extremely sizable, and so was the cistern. The original working cistern was along the western side of the house. It was formed by large blocks and was subdivided with a low wall midway across it. My husband explained that old cisterns typically collected water from the roof. The water would enter one side of the cistern, and sediment would settle out. Water that was relatively free of sediment would then flow over the low wall so that the water drawn for household use would be clearer and purer. This first cistern conformed to that basic plan and was the design of a typical old-style cistern. You could peek over the wall and see the large pool-like interior.

At the other side of the building, on the eastern side, was the false cistern, which in no way conformed to nineteenth-century cistern design or any other type of cistern design. The first thing that was noticeable about this cistern was that it was higher than the other, so it was not as easy to see inside. The wall went to a certain height that perhaps would have been normal for a cistern and then arched away as it climbed higher. The cistern's outer wall was twelve inches thick, similar to the actual cistern. It took a six-foot ladder to climb over the top of the cistern. The false cistern was seventy-two inches long, but the back basement stairs covered part of its length.

The second unusual feature of this cistern is that it was only eighteen inches from the support wall of the building at the bottom and sixteen inches from the wall at the top. Those measurements are from the inside of the cistern blocks to the flagstone wall of the house. The top of the cistern was quite close to the basement ceiling. In order to get into the cistern, we climbed the ladder, laid ourselves flat on the top of the cistern and shimmied our way around. There was not much room to maneuver between the top of the cistern and the ceiling beams or between the wall of the cistern and the building support wall. Further complicating things was a metal bar that was between the wall of the building and the cistern wall. All of this left us shifting around like amateur contortionists trying to get in. Someone had left a chair at the bottom of the cistern, which was obviously placed so that a person could get back out by standing on the chair and grasping the metal bar to pull himself out.

A built-in metal bar spans the false cistern and can be used to climb out. *Photo courtesy of Francis Zimmer.*

I finally maneuvered around and lowered myself down, feet first onto the chair and then stepped onto the floor. A small archway was on the floor of the cistern in the support wall of the building. At its apex, it measured twenty-two inches high. There was some wood beneath and around it. If this had ever contained water, wood would not be a natural selection for an opening at the bottom of a cistern. Beneath the archway was a six-inch ledge of wood. We could not determine why it had been put there. The tiny tunnel or entranceway was twenty-six inches in length. I crawled through it, though it wasn't easy as the cistern was only eighteen inches wide, so there was really no room for my backside to align behind me as I crawled through the tiny tunnel. What little room there was was already filled with the chair. Still, I managed to get through the entrance and found myself in a small brick-lined room with a wooden ceiling.

The room was quite dirty, and the floor was gritty and had gravel on it. There was a dead animal in there, though I can vouch that it had simply died in place and no one had made a meal of it. It appeared to have been a rabbit. The room was short. You could comfortably sit or kneel, but I am five 5'9", so I could not have stood there. It was only 62 inches high, so a person

Ceiling of the hidden room behind the cistern. *Photo courtesy of Francis Zimmer*

A look into the crawl space that leads to the secret room concealed behind the cistern. *Photo courtesy of Francis Zimmer.*

The author entering the hidden room behind the cistern. *Photo courtesy of Francis Zimmer.*

just under 5 feet and 2 inches could have stood there, just gazing at the ceiling. The distance from the end of the tunnel to the back of the room was 69 inches (almost 5.8 feet). If that is considered the length of the room, then the width is 61.5 inches (or 5.1 feet). The walls of the room were constructed of brick, but strangely, there was a plaster coating over the brick that began approximately 2 feet off the floor and went to the ceiling. This coating in many places appeared blackish. Smoke can be a possible reason for blacking on walls that does not appear at the bottom. As smoke rises, it deposits soot only several feet above the source. I do not know if the black material was soot. I cannot explain why anyone would coat the top of the brick walls in a supposed cistern but not the bottom when it would be the bottom that fills first and should be impermeable to water. The first and functioning cistern had a layer of plaster-like material over the blocks, but it was everywhere, not just at the top. This and the overall structure made no sense for a cistern designed to hold water. There was no other exit from the cistern but the tiny tunnel, through which we had entered the tiny room. Rumors of a tunnel that exited onto Peterboro Road were false. Even before entering the cistern, we questioned how it would have been possible to tunnel so far as Peterboro Road, let alone to add such a structure after the construction of the house.

This false cistern could have functioned as a hiding place. Certainly, once a person was inside, it would be difficult to detect the person's presence. The stairs from the basement to the back of the pantry went right over one side of the fake cistern, making it even more inaccessible. This staircase was at the back of the house, and if someone were coming, a person (such as a fugitive slave) could have run down the back stairs to hide in the cistern.

Having said that, I would also have to say this hiding place would not be suitable for husky individuals, the injured, elder persons or pregnant women. Any person hiding in such a location would ideally be young, healthy, thin and limber. If a person were in hiding there, it would be easy for an accomplice to come down the back steps and drop food into the cistern unnoticed. There appeared to be a root cellar nearby, so a servant slipping into the basement would be natural. I did not descend into the cistern quickly, which could have been problematic, but then a shorter individual may have had less difficulty. And because it is so difficult to descend into the secret room, it would have been less likely to have been located by law enforcement or vigilantes. In truth, there is no hard evidence that the false cistern was used to hide humans (or more specifically, fugitive slaves), only suggestion. It may well have been used to hide possessions, although the Jenkins house was teeming with servants, so it seems odd to me that he would hide valuable possessions without the use of lock or key in a basement that was readily available to his household staff.

The Jenkins house took two years to build and was not created with nonfunctioning features. Family records tell that when the beams in the house were installed, Jenkins would jump on them. If they did not pass muster, if they wavered ever so slightly, then he insisted that they be strengthened. Jenkins was not the kind of man who would install a nonworking cistern or a poor cistern without a reason.

Edith Monsour told me a story that was related to her by a relative of Mr. Jenkins. One day, Mr. Jenkins was driving his carriage in Vernon, and another driver tried to pass him. Mr. Jenkins then took his whip and whipped the driver of the other carriage in the face. The driver, injured, went into a local tavern and found the law enforcement agent to tell him what had happened. He described the man who had whipped him. He suddenly saw Mr. Jenkins and pointed him out. "There he is!" he cried.

"Well," said the police officer, "if he is the one who hit you, then you deserved it."

Edith tells this story to suggest that the police were in Mr. Jenkins's pocket. I tell it to suggest that Mr. Jenkins was unlikely to have had local law enforcement agents combing through his home (although federal agents might still have been a possibility). He was apparently a powerful man in Vernon, and as such, his home would have been one of the safer places to hide fleeing slaves from the law. There appears to be no written evidence that Mr. Jenkins did more than fight legal battles for men like Mr. John Brown. We do not know with any certainty if he actually hid slaves, or if he or his family were an active part of the Underground Railroad, although, with his connections to others who were active in moving slaves toward freedom, it would hardly have been surprising.

John Brown. *Courtesy of the Library of Congress.*

JOSIAH WHIPPLE JENKINS, ESQ., JOHN BROWN AND ABOLITIONIST GERRIT SMITH

The home's builder, Josiah Whipple Jenkins, was born in Barr, Massachusetts, and was the eldest son of a large family. He taught school as a young man, but after a year in the classroom, he left teaching to join his cousin, Timothy Jenkins, at his law practice in Vernon. Timothy Jenkins was the attorney for abolitionist Gerrit Smith. Josiah Whipple became the attorney for John Brown, known for his attack on Harper's Ferry. Gerrit Smith, a wealthy man and philanthropist, as well as strong reformer and abolitionist, partially funded John Brown's attack on Harper's Ferry.

Not long after Josiah Jenkins had passed the bar exam, Timothy Jenkins moved his practice to Oneida Castle, and Josiah Jenkins continued to operate from Vernon. Jenkins's connection to the Smith family went beyond that legal association. Josiah Jenkins's wife, Electra Tuttle, was the child of Captain and Mrs. David Tuttle. Though the couple originally hailed from Connecticut, they moved to Madison County, New York. It was there that Electra was born on June 18, 1813. Judge Smith, Gerrit Smith's father, was the one who recommended that the Tuttles move to Smithfield. Though the family only lived there for perhaps a year and a half, this shows that both the Jenkins family and Electra's family, the Tuttles, were connected to the Smiths of Peterboro.

It is worth noting that both Josiah Jenkins and his wife were active Unitarians in Vernon. There were strong connections to the abolitionist

Stereoscopic view of the engine house fortified by John Brown at Harper's Ferry, VA. Courtesy of the Library of Congress.

movement among some Unitarian churches. Minister Samuel Joseph May, for instance, was active in the Jerry Rescue, and two Unitarians belonged to the Secret Six who funded Harper's Ferry.

Gerrit Smith was the son of Peter Smith, a man whose immense wealth came from both his property holdings as well as his success in the fur trade with his partner John Jacob Astor. Not long after Gerrit graduated as valedictorian from Hamilton College, his father looked to him to take over the family land office, despite Gerrit's own wishes. Gerrit had a brother, but he was thought to be mentally incompetent and not suitable to take over the business. Gerrit soon established himself as a businessman in Peterboro, New York. Using the vast resources that were primarily accumulated by his father, Gerrit Smith, in addition to running the land office, also became a major philanthropic force in New York and in the nation.

One of Gerrit Smith's most unique philanthropic programs was begun in 1846, when Smith announced he intended to subdivide 120,000 acres of land in the Adirondacks in Essex County into lots that would be given to black males for the purpose of farming, in order to make them landholders. In April 1848, abolitionist John Brown approached Gerrit and asked for land so that he might live among the blacks who were settling there and aid them by teaching them basic farming skills. Brown had heard of Gerrit through his own father, who was a trustee at Oberlin College and who knew of Gerrit's abolitionist leanings. Smith did not hesitate to sell 244 acres of land to Brown in North Elba, Essex County, in the vicinity of Lake Placid, for $244, an extraordinarily low price at that time. This encounter became the first in a long association between

Gerrit Smith. *Courtesy of the Library of Congress.*

Hamilton College, Gerrit Smith's alma mater. *Courtesy of the Library of Congress.*

The Peterboro Land Office, located on the right, was where Gerrit Smith worked, and it stood next to the Smith estate. It has since burned down. *Photo courtesy of the author.*

Brown and Smith. John Brown lived on that land in North Elba from 1849 to 1851. In 1855, John Brown moved to Kansas to continue his abolitionist activities and received funding for his activities from Smith. Smith began spending heavily, trying to relocate people to Kansas so that the state would be established as a free state, spending as much as $1,000 a month on some occasions for that purpose. More than that, Smith was funding Brown's activities in Kansas, which were quite violent. Smith's money was used by

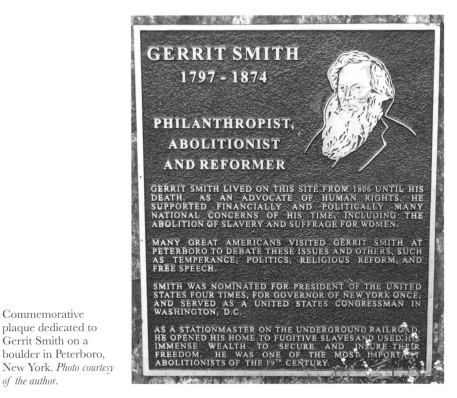

GERRIT SMITH
1797 - 1874

PHILANTHROPIST,
ABOLITIONIST
AND REFORMER

GERRIT SMITH LIVED ON THIS SITE FROM 1806 UNTIL HIS
DEATH. AS AN ADVOCATE OF HUMAN RIGHTS, HE
SUPPORTED FINANCIALLY AND POLITICALLY MANY
NATIONAL CONCERNS OF HIS TIME, INCLUDING THE
ABOLITION OF SLAVERY AND SUFFRAGE FOR WOMEN.

MANY GREAT AMERICANS VISITED GERRIT SMITH AT
PETERBORO TO DEBATE THESE ISSUES AND OTHERS, SUCH
AS TEMPERANCE, POLITICS, RELIGIOUS REFORM, AND
FREE SPEECH.

SMITH WAS NOMINATED FOR PRESIDENT OF THE UNITED
STATES FOUR TIMES, FOR GOVERNOR OF NEW YORK ONCE,
AND SERVED AS A UNITED STATES CONGRESSMAN IN
WASHINGTON, D.C.

AS A STATIONMASTER ON THE UNDERGROUND RAILROAD,
HE OPENED HIS HOME TO FUGITIVE SLAVES AND USED HIS
IMMENSE WEALTH TO SECURE AND INSURE THEIR
FREEDOM. HE WAS ONE OF THE MOST IMPORTANT
ABOLITIONISTS OF THE 19TH CENTURY.

Commemorative plaque dedicated to Gerrit Smith on a boulder in Peterboro, New York. *Photo courtesy of the author.*

Brown to buy arms. Once Governor Geary called federal troops into Kansas, Brown redirected his efforts to Virginia, (now West Virginia) developing the plan for his attack on Harper's Ferry.

Remarkably, John Brown was able to convince several benefactors to back his planned attack. The purpose of the attack would be to take weapons from the arsenal and armory and then use them to establish a base in the Appalachian Mountains to attack plantations in an effort to free slaves. The idea seems a bit far-fetched, and John Brown did not have a long history of success on which to stand. Still, he was able to obtain financial backing from several abolitionists who became known as the "Secret Six." Gerrit Smith was one of those men.

The members of the Secret Six were two Unitarian ministers, Thomas Wentworth Higginson and Theodore Parker; a young teacher from Massachusetts named Franklin Benjamin Sanborn; a doctor from Boston named Samuel Gridley Howe; a merchant named George Luther Stearns who was also from Boston; and, of course, Gerrit Smith.

Although Gerrit Smith had apparently stated that he did not wish to know how John Brown used the money he sent him, Gerrit Smith was nonetheless

Left: Colonel T.W. Higginson was one of the "Secret Six" who funded the raid on Harper's Ferry. William Notman. *Courtesy of the Library of Congress.*

Below: Wood engraving of Theodore Parker lecturing in New York. Parker was one of the Secret Six. *Courtesy of the Library of Congress.*

The interior of the engine house at Harper's Ferry, just before the gate was broken down. *Courtesy of the Library of Congress.*

intricately involved in the planning for the raid on Harper's Ferry. Over the course of two days, February 22 and 23, 1858, John Brown, Sanborn and Edwin Morton discussed plans for the attack. Subsequently, Brown traveled to Boston where he held meetings with the other members of the Secret Six regarding the plans. Brown also met with escaped slave Fredrick Douglass, a Syracuse man named Jermain Loguen (Loguen was instrumental in the Jerry Rescue in Syracuse) and Harriet Tubman. Tubman, who lived in Auburn, New York, had brought numerous

Harriet Tubman. *Courtesy of the Library of Congress.*

slaves north on the Underground Railroad and has been heralded as its most successful conductor.

The raid itself took place on Sunday, October 16, 1859, when Brown and twenty-one others attacked the arsenal at Harper's Ferry. One of the attack's goals was to gain weaponry to liberate slaves. However, U.S. Marines quickly put down the attack on the arsenal. Ten of Brown's men died. Brown himself was tried for treason and executed on December 2, 1859. Others in Brown's party were also tried, found guilty and executed.

The apprehension, trial and execution of John Brown were psychologically destructive to Gerrit Smith, and the damage to his reputation was irreversible. Where Smith had once garnered approval from at least a segment of the population for his abolitionist and reform philanthropies, Smith's association with the treasonous attack changed everything. And the evidence against him was extraordinary. A letter from Smith to Brown dated June 4, 1859, and a $100 bank draft that Smith had sent to help fund the raid were found among Brown's belongings. Furthermore, there was a letter that Brown had written that implicated Smith as one of the financiers in the raid and the subsequent slave rebellion that was meant to follow.

The newspapers were full of accusations regarding Smith's involvement in financing the raid. Many believed that Smith's actions were just as treasonous as Brown's attack. Several of the other financiers fled the country, and Smith's attorney, Timothy Jenkins, recommended that Smith do the same.

Wood engraving entitled *En Route for Harper's Ferry*, 1859. *Courtesy of the Library of Congress.*

A panoramic view of soldiers surrounding gallows, from which two of the Harper's Ferry Raiders are hanging. Wood engraving, 1859. *Courtesy of the Library of Congress.*

Wood engraving by Arthur Berghaus depicting John Brown riding on his coffin to the place of his execution, 1859. *Courtesy of the Library of Congress.*

John Brown's execution, near Charleston, West Virginia. *Courtesy of the Library of Congress.*

According to various accounts, Smith reportedly became very agitated and his behavior erratic, presumably due to incredible stress. Smith did not, however, flee the country. Instead, he seemed to have a complete lapse of sanity and was committed to New York State Lunatic Asylum in Utica on November 7, 1859, by those close to him. That move was very controversial, and many people believed that Smith entered the Lunatic Asylum to avoid extradition to Virginia. In fact, one would presume with Smith still in the country and located at a known facility, that extradition would still be likely. The authorities agreed, however, that he was indeed, a lunatic.

While some say that Smith was trying to evade justice, ample evidence of mental health issues within the Smith family suggests that the event was all that was needed to push Smith over the edge. Previously, Smith's brother, Peter Skenendoah Smith, had been committed to an asylum, though apparently he later recovered. Some have suggested Smith's father had also suffered from some form of mental instability in his later years. Even Smith's son, Greene, exhibited behaviors suggestive of possible mental illness. Furthermore, Gerrit Smith had embraced some unusual philanthropy over the years in giving land to free blacks and funding abolitionist activity in Kansas, and some pointed to this as evidence of his inherently unbalanced mind. Whatever the reason, according to reports, Smith was unable to sleep

Sign for the Utica Insane Asylum, historically known as the New York State Lunatic Asylum. *Courtesy of the author.*

The Utica Insane Asylum. *Courtesy of the author.*

and suffered from extreme agitation as well as hallucinations during his stay at the asylum. He was given marijuana as a calming agent and also morphine, such was his state. He was ordered to rest and placed on a special diet. Smith was released after fifty-two days of treatment. This, too, led to speculation that his insanity had been merely a ploy to avoid prosecution and possible execution. Even after his short stay in Utica, Smith was not sent to trial in Virginia, though it is said that immediately after Brown's capture, he had set about destroying letters that implicated his role in the plot, so one must presume he was in possession of his faculties immediately following the failed raid.

Gerrit Smith denied involvement with the raid until the day he died, despite all evidence to the contrary. He claimed his funding was not destined for a raid, but rather for other activities. In fact, Smith even had the audacity to sue the *Chicago Tribune* for suggesting that he had been a knowing participant in the funding of the raid.

THE BROWN DONKEYS IN VERNON

According to an old newspaper article entitled "John Brown in Vernon," John Brown frequented the village, and Mr. Josiah Whipple Jenkins provided him with legal services for several years. Obviously, Mr. Jenkins died long before the attack on Harper's Ferry. Mr. Brown would often come to stay for a week or ten days before one of his cases was scheduled to be heard in court. According to the same source, Brown first hired Josiah Jenkins while Mr. Brown was living in Essex County. In later days, when Brown moved to Akron, Ohio, four or five of Brown's sons would travel to Vernon in a wagon pulled by four yoked oxen and three donkeys. This variety of transport could not have been very fast, but the animals were stabled in the Jenkins's barn, and the donkeys were a tremendous hit among young Vernon residents. In fact, on one occasion, an entire group of school children came to visit the donkeys. The donkeys were brought out of the barn onto the expansive lawn. So alluring were the donkeys that the school boys wanted to ride them, and they did try. One by one, a number of school boys would mount a donkey, but the beast would have none of it. The donkey would simply shake itself, and each boy would slide right off. That donkey knew who was really in charge.

The World's Smallest Church

Though I had lived close by for the last twenty years, I did not discover the world's smallest church until I found myself lost one day, having taken a wrong turn. I knew it was a wrong turn as I discovered I most definitely was not heading toward town. To my right was a small pond, and there was a small chapel in its center that appeared to almost float. The chapel was so tiny that it appeared to be the size of a modest play house. On the shore was a sign that read "Welcome to the Oneida, N.Y. home of Cross Island Chapel, World's Smallest Chapel."

One might just wonder how on heaven or earth it would be possible to hold a wedding ceremony in a church so very tiny, for the chapel is only big enough to hold a minister, a bride and a groom. But when a wedding does occur, the guests are seated in small boats or on the nearby shoreline, as the pond is quite small as well. A seat on shore must be closer than some would have in a massive cathedral. For those just stopping by to view the chapel, some patriotic Adirondack chairs are conveniently provided near the sign.

Cross Island Chapel. *Photo courtesy of the author.*

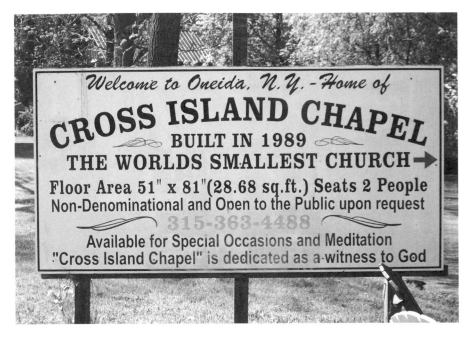

The sign at Cross Island Chapel. *Photo courtesy of the author.*

Cross Island Chapel takes its name from an island that is formed by a small pile of rocks that peek above the waterline nearby, supporting a large cross. The chapel itself is supported by wooden pylons and a very petite deck that stands quite close to the surface of the water. The church is accessible by a rowboat, which is provided by the caretaker.

The chapel is a simple rectangular white clapboard building with a small steeple. It has a single door and two stained glass windows that depict the Holy Spirit. The inside of the chapel is paneled in light wood, and it contains four chairs that might seem a bit small for most adults. While the chapel lacks an altar, it does contain a pulpit. Weddings and services have been held there, but there is no minister or congregation specifically associated with the chapel; rather, the users make their own arrangements. As the church is nondenominational, it may be used for a variety of types of services, and there is no charge, though those interested should contact the caretaker. It is definitely a church for worshipers who enjoy solitude, the stillness of the water and spending time alone with God.

The chapel is located on Sconandoa Road in Oneida, New York. Sconondoa Road is accessible from Route 365.

THE SPIRIT HOUSE

In the small community of Georgetown, there stands a remarkable building just off Route 26 that goes by a number of names: the Spirit House, the Wedding Cake House, the Timothy Brown House, Brown's Free Hall and Brown's Temple. The building is stunning and covered with the most extraordinary fretwork as the descriptive name "Wedding Cake House" implies. Even with its peeling paint, the structure still prompts travelers to pull off the road to study its unique architecture. But what really fascinates people is not the house itself but the story of its creation by a man named Timothy Brown.

According to the January 18, 1879 edition of a Spiritualist periodical called the *Banner of Light*, Timothy Brown, a middle-aged farmer, sold his land, moved to Georgetown and purchased new land for himself and his wife, Sarah. One night, as he lay awake contemplating building a new home, he was confronted by several mysterious images of houses. These images stood in the air before him, and he studied each carefully, at last settling on the design that would become the house known today as the Spirit House. This image then reappeared to him several times, and it became embedded

Exterior of the Spirit House today. *Photo courtesy of the author.*

Interior scalloped doorway of the Timothy Brown House from the 1966 Historic American Buildings Survey. *Courtesy of the Library of Congress.*

in his memory. Brown believed these images had come from his dead sister Mary, so he cried out, "If this is Mary, let her open the bedroom door!"

As he watched, the door swung gently open, and a glowing mist appeared before him. The mist parted, and there stood a lovely woman, but she quickly vanished. Brown believed from that moment he was destined to build the house, so he purchased a nearby lot and set about felling timber. Legend tells that Brown was not a carpenter, an architect or a mason, but he nonetheless worked consistently on the house, laboring long hours while his wife, Sarah, worked as a cheese maker.

The spirits guided his every move. It was said that if he held his chisel in the wrong place, he would find himself helpless to strike it. If, however, he held it where the blows were meant to be made, his arm moved easily. In this way, he was guided to follow the design of the spirits. The townspeople frequently ridiculed Brown for his folly and his odd design, and an unusual design it was.

The home Timothy Brown built in Georgetown prior to building the Spirit House. Despite tales of Brown's inexperience in building, he exhibited skilled carpentry work on his prior home, just down the road in Georgetown. *Photo courtesy of the author.*

In Central New York, most people prefer pitched roofs so that the snow will slide off, eliminating snow weight from their homes. Brown's construction, however, featured the reverse. According to a March 19, 1896 article in the *DeRuyter Gleaner* called "Spiritual Temple," Brown was seen shingling his house inside out. He made a concave roof where the water from rain and snow would run through a central pipe right through the second floor, down to the basement and into a cistern. Even today, the strange structure of circular support beams can be seen on the ceiling of the second story, radiating out from a central hole. Not long ago, however, there was a leak that caused severe damage, and many rooms had to be gutted. The interior walls will likely be replaced by drywall. Admittedly, this occurred during a time when the house stood vacant, and perhaps it could have been prevented had the house been in use and well maintained. Today, the roof has been repaired by shingling over the concave roof, and the original structure is no longer apparent from the outside, though the beam support structure still exists on the second floor ceiling.

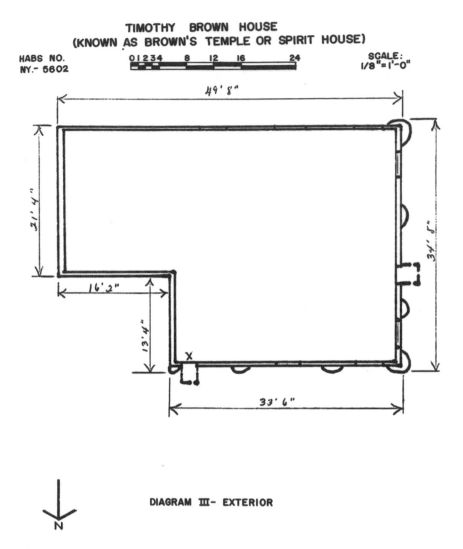

TIMOTHY BROWN HOUSE
(KNOWN AS BROWN'S TEMPLE OR SPIRIT HOUSE)

HABS NO.
NY.- 5602

0 1 2 3 4   8   12   16   24

SCALE:
1/8"=1'-0"

49' 8"

31' 4"

34' 8"

16' 2"

13' 4"

X

33' 6"

DIAGRAM III- EXTERIOR

N

Undated sketch plan of the exterior of the Timothy Brown House. From the Historic American Buildings Survey. *Courtesy of the Library of Congress.*

The townspeople believed this design was faulty (there was even a rumor the roof was designed to funnel spirits into the spirit closets) and that the roof would become clogged by snow in the wintertime. However, when the first snows came, people gathered round to watch, and to their amazement, they saw snow accumulating on the neighboring rooftops, but swirls of wind brought the falling snow gently away from Brown's roof, leaving no accumulation at all.

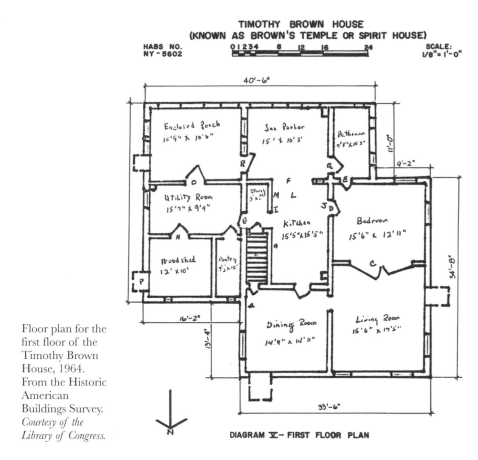

TIMOTHY BROWN HOUSE
(KNOWN AS BROWN'S TEMPLE OR SPIRIT HOUSE)

HABS NO.
NY - 5602

SCALE:
1/8"= 1'-0"

Floor plan for the
first floor of the
Timothy Brown
House, 1964.
From the Historic
American
Buildings Survey.
*Courtesy of the
Library of Congress.*

DIAGRAM Ⅴ— FIRST FLOOR PLAN

The roof design was not the only defining feature of the house or even the most remarkable. What first strikes the eye when a viewer sees the Spirit House are the three tiers of incredible sculpted eves. Their decorative details have been compared to inverted clock keys and icicles, but they really defy description. And though the entire structure today is painted white, it was originally red, white and blue. One must see the eaves to understand them, and it is perhaps impossible even then. For Timothy Brown, the architectural details were secondary to the function of the eves. These were special eves. They were designed to be "spirit closets," or structures designed to house spirits. One presumes they were comfortable and to the liking of the spirits, if the house was indeed designed and the building supervised by them.

It is one thing to have spirits nesting in closets around your home but quite another to have hostile or evil spirits residing there. To avoid that possibility, Brown placed molding with rounded nicked designs everywhere.

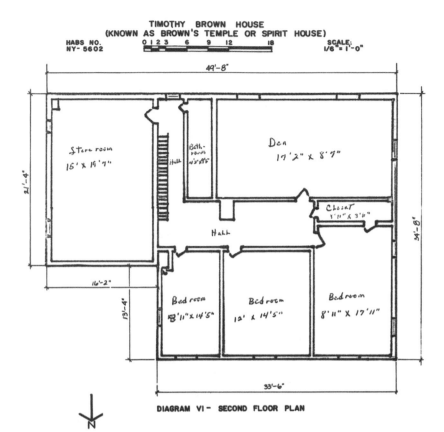

TIMOTHY BROWN HOUSE
(KNOWN AS BROWN'S TEMPLE OR SPIRIT HOUSE)
HABS NO.
NY- 5602

SCALE:
1/6" = 1'-0"

DIAGRAM VI - SECOND FLOOR PLAN

Above: Floor plan for the second floor of the Timothy Brown House, 1964. From the Historic American Buildings Survey. *Courtesy of the Library of Congress.*

Left: Recent interior view of the Spirit House. The interior of the house was gutted due to water damage from a leaking roof, and much of the interior wood work that was covered with scallops, presumably to protect against evil spirits, was lost. *Photo courtesy of the author.*

Spirit closets and exterior cornice detail of the Timothy Brown House, 1966. From the Historic American Buildings Survey. *Courtesy of the Library of Congress.*

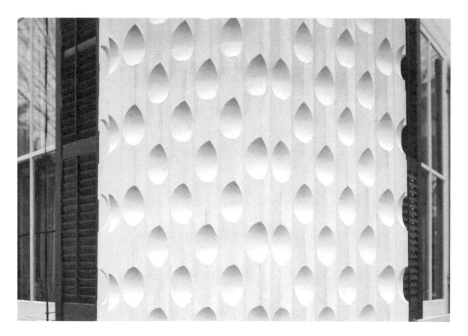

The exterior corner column of the Timothy Brown House shows the scallops thought to prevent evil spirits from inhabiting the house. From the Historic American Buildings Survey. *Courtesy of the Library of Congress.*

The outside of the house is stunning in part because of the unusual texture of the building created by the nicks. The scalloped design was also a bold feature on molding surrounding doorways and window frames. The theory was that evil spirits could abide in square corners but never in rounded ones. Thus, the Spirit House became a residence for benign spirits.

Also included in the house was an unusual room, known as "the dark room," said to be a space where spirits were conjured or a place where spirits could rest. Others say it was a space where mediums could work. Structurally, it was an interior room downstairs without windows. Madis Senner, who led the recent attempt to purchase the house to restore it and use it as a spiritual retreat, used a bent piece of metal to demonstrate that this room was an energy center. He took a bent rod and walked the length of the room. At a certain point, the rod began spinning rapidly. According to Senner, the rod's spinning demonstrated the presence of energy vortexes, which made the house a great place for a spiritual retreat. These vortexes

Detail from the outside of the Spirit House today. *Photo courtesy of the author.*

Above: The woodwork surrounding the porch also shows scallop work. *Photo courtesy of the author*.

Right: The grounds surrounding the Spirit House are said to emanate good feelings due to vortexes located on the property. *Photo courtesy of the author*.

Out building on the property of the Spirit House. *Photo courtesy of the author.*

The Timothy Brown House, or Spirit House, 1966. From the Historic American Buildings Survey. *Courtesy of the Library of Congress.*

explain the blissful feeling of happiness one finds in that location. Senner located another vortex in one of the outbuildings as well. According to an anonymous article from the *Cazenovia Republican* dated November 18, 1933, Brown kept a single chair in the dark room and used the space to personally communicate with the spirits.

The entire upstairs of the house was an auditorium, and theatrical events were held there. A variety of events were held at the Spirit House, and not all of them were intimately connected to the spirit world. People came to see the Spirit House from near and far. Because of its immense popularity, Brown decided to expand in 1874, adding a Presbyterian church to the back of the house. Around 1840, the Presbyterian Church split over the slavery issue. The abolitionists formed the Free Methodist Church, and after the Civil War, the original church building was unneeded. Brown bought the church and used it as a handy ready-made addition to his Spirit House. With the addition, Brown could seat six hundred people, and the new addition also contained a raised stage for performances.

A wide variety of programming was held at The Spirit House. There were lectures and plays. A play bill for a musical rendition of *Uncle Tom's Cabin* that was performed by the West Eaton Troup on December 17, 1880, still exists. At one point, there was a trial held in the Spirit House when the expected crowd exceeded the capacity of the courthouse. In addition, each year, during the 1870s and 1880s, the Central New York Association of Spiritualists held its annual picnic at the Spirit House around the time of the September equinox.

The Spirit House has recently been purchased by a private individual who hopes to begin work on restoring or repairing the structure. The owner has spoken of the possibility of opening the house to the public at a later date.

THE MYSTERY OF THE MULLER CHÂTEAU

Located in what is now a state park in the small village of Georgetown are the remnants of the château that was owned by a man who went by the name of Louis Anathe Muller. Little remains of the château now except a few pits that used to serve as basements, and even these have been almost consumed by the surrounding woods, leaving little evidence of the small village that stood there or the mystery that surrounded it and the man called Louis Muller. To this very day, no one can say with certainty who Muller really was.

This pit is one of the few remains of the Muller Mansion. *Courtesy of the author.*

In 1808, Louis Muller purchased 2,700 acres of wilderness on what is today called Muller Hill in Georgetown, New York. Georgetown is a tiny village today, not much bigger than it was then. Muller purchased the land from Daniel Ludlow of New York City.

Carrying with him a letter of introduction from Mr. Ludlow, Mr. Muller took up temporary residence for about a year in Hamilton, New York, a village eight miles from his purchased property, while his home was constructed. The finished product was astonishing to local residents. The home was considered a mansion in itself, but the reality was that Mr. Muller had constructed an entire village in the wilderness, and it was occupied by a large staff of French servants that he had brought with him to this country.

Muller's magnificent residence was seventy feet long and thirty feet wide and was situated on the highest hill in Georgetown. It was constructed of cherry beams from virgin wood that had been cut from the hillside itself, and the walls were of a remarkable thickness, varying between ten and eighteen inches in depth. The building was strong as any fortress, with sturdy masonry, and the woods were cleared to reveal a distant view. Many called it a perfect stronghold, and Muller was known to surrounded himself with liverymen who were armed with guns whenever he traveled. Many suggested that the mysterious Louis Muller was a man in hiding.

The site had two streams located nearby, and a pond was created and stocked with fish. Muller had a gristmill and a sawmill constructed. A storehouse and two stores also sprung up on his property. Housing was added for the servants, and there was an enclosed park where Muller hunted game with a gun, as was his custom. It was said Muller employed 150 people on Muller Hill.

The mansion was remarkable in both its size and its location. The one-story house had six fireplaces and three chimneys. It is said the fireplaces were faced with black marble. The outside of the home was clapboard and the inside plaster and lathe. The furniture was fine in quality, with many costly pieces having been imported from Europe. The house contained both an attic and a cellar. A long hall ran through the center of the building, dividing the house in two. On one side were four connected rooms, and on the other side was the kitchen with its pantries, a dining room and a stairway.

The lake on top of Muller Hill. There is a lake on top of Muller Hill that may have been created by Muller as a mill pond. The lake on top of Muller Hill was greatly expanded many decades ago. This is how it appears today. *Courtesy of the author.*

The House on Muller Hill by Dwight Williams, circa 1884. The Muller home burned down in 1905. The painting is on display at the Georgetown Historical Society. *Photo courtesy of the author.*

Photograph of the Muller Mansion. *Courtesy of the Georgetown Historical Society.*

Muller's yard was landscaped with pathways, plantings and statues. This surely was a remarkable home to occupy such a small village, and nobody nearby could have been as wealthy or mysterious as Muller was.

Above: Front view of a model of the Muller Mansion on display at the Georgetown Historical Society. *Photo courtesy of the author.*

Right: Side view of a model of the Muller Mansion on display at the Georgetown Historical Society. *Photo courtesy of the author.*

An interior view of a model of the Muller Mansion on display at the Georgetown Historical Society. *Photo courtesy of the author.*

It was here that the man known as Louis Anathe Muller made his home with his wife and daughter. A second daughter was later born at their new home.

As it was not every day that a Frenchman arrived in a tiny remote village with an entire retinue of French servants and constructed a mansion and a village for his own usage, the locals naturally wondered who this mysterious man was. As a rule, Muller kept his own confidence, leading Georgetown villagers and those living in the countryside to speculate as to what Muller's true identity might be.

Several things are known about this man. He was a martinet, demanding rigid adherence to his words and instructions. He did not hesitate to fire workmen he did not find satisfactory, and he was litigious. Thomas H. Hubbard served as his lawyer, and Hubbard's services were frequently required as Muller flooded the local courts with cases involving inadequate workmanship and matters of payments made to hired hands. Muller made few friends and kept to himself and his family, which made him all the more mysterious to the people.

He was described as a small man, about five feet five inches tall and around fifty years old. He had a dark complexion and black eyes. His features were sharp, and he carried himself with an air of authority, culture and refinement. He had what appeared to be a military presence.

Besides the servants that accompanied him from France, he employed local people and encouraged skilled workers to settle in his village. Some even say he was a kind man; others disagree.

In Georgetown, Muller tried his hand at farming, though it was soon obvious that he knew little about cultivating the land, planting seeds and the like. At one point it was recorded that he bought so many turnip seeds that he could have drowned the entire town in turnips.

He bore an extreme distaste for Napoleon Bonaparte and followed his doings in Europe, speaking of him with disgust. For this reason, some believed that Muller had fled Napoleon. In fact, it was when Napoleon marched on Russia in 1812 that Muller began to believe that Napoleon's army would be defeated. Sensing an impending loss, Muller returned to Europe toward the

Napoleon Bonaparte.
Courtesy of the Library of Congress.

end of 1813 or in 1814. He left his property in the hands of an agent and left his wife and daughters there as well to await his return. However, when Muller did return in 1816, he discovered that the agent had sold many of his possessions while he was away. Little more than the building's structures in various states of disrepair remained upon his return. His village was found deserted, and Muller, in disgust, sold the property to Abijah Weston for the price of $10,500. Muller left once again for France, this time with his family, never to return to Georgetown. The mysterious disappearance of Muller only added to his mystique.

Rumors and theories of who Muller really was began to fly. Different people offered various theories on Muller's true identity. Surely, some thought, he was a French nobleman who was forced to flee from Napoleon. Why else would he choose to return to his homeland so suddenly upon Napoleon's defeat? Some thought, given his military bearing, that he was a French general. Some believed he might have been a guard or a general of the king. Others thought he was Charles X, known in his earlier life as the Comte d'Artois. Still others imagined he was the son of Charles X, Charles Ferdinand, Duke of Berry. Another line of thought identifies Muller as Louis Philippe.

According to an 1893 paper by Robert J. Hubbard, after the assassination of the Duke of Enghien in 1804, the French nobility felt threatened and fled to a variety of safe havens, realizing there would be no coexistence with Napoleon. Many fled to England, but the threat of assassination still loomed large, so others sought safety in America, living in cognito. Louis Anathe Muller was believed to be such a man in hiding.

Muller's military bearing and his strong disciplinarian ways supported another theory that he was a general of the old French regime. Muller demanded obedience, and those who showed obedience and performed their labors as prescribed were rewarded. Loafers and shoddy workmen were promptly dismissed and had no promise of ever being rehired. But these are general characteristics. Muller confided in few, and in those few trusted individuals, he said little to shed light on his secret identity. There was one man Muller did trust: Chancellor Bierce. Bierce worked for Muller for a period of three years, and the two grew somewhat close, though it must be said that Muller was want to expose his identity to anyone. During this time, Muller was called to military training. He refused and, by all accounts, was extremely insulted by being asked to train. Bierce later recalled that Muller told him, "Mr. Bierce, it is too bad! Too bad! Captain Hurd sends his corporal to warn *me* out to train! He ought to be ashamed! I have been

General of a division five years! I have signed three treaties." At that point, Muller stopped himself, perhaps aware he had said too much.

Though Bierce went on to explain to him the rules regarding military training, Muller refused to answer the call as long as he resided in Georgetown. Muller made it a point to never discuss his knowledge of French military affairs. But, when Napoleon and his 450,000 troops began the march on Russia, Muller was said to have exclaimed "He shall be whipped; he shall be driven back!" And indeed, Napoleon suffered extraordinary losses, limping home with an army that had been reduced to 100,000. Muller seemed to have understood the trap of advancing on Russia and immediately made plans for his return to French soil.

Though many believed Louis Muller's real identity was Charles X, King of France, very little evidence exists to make that case. The story goes that after the Duke of Enghien was assassinated, many members of the French aristocracy went into exile, fearing for their safety, Charles X included. Charles X fled to London. However, even though he no longer dwelled in France, his personal safety was still not assured, and some supposed that it would have made sense to venture to an isolated location in America and live under an assumed name until such time as the danger in Europe subsided. According to the story, in 1797, at Holyrood Castle, the Count was dogged by creditors. As long as he remained within the castle, he was protected by the law, and they could not reach him. He could only leave the castle grounds on Sundays. For these reasons, it is said, the Count of Artois may have preferred the anonymity of American rural life.

One reason that the Duke of Berry is suspected of being identical to Muller is because the duke married a woman named Amy Brown and lived with her for ten years. This marriage produced two daughters, Charlotte and Louise, who spoke English. (The pope later annulled the marriage.) Two different accounts of Louis Muller's marriage exist. In one, he was believed to have brought an American wife whose name was Stuyvesant to Georgetown. In the other version, he married an English woman named Amy Brown in 1806 and brought her to Georgetown. He had two daughters by the time he sold his Georgetown property. Some believed the duke and Muller possibly having a wife of the same name, and also two daughters by their respective wives, could be more than coincidence.

When Louis Philippe wandered in Europe during his exile, he feared for his own safety. He traveled under different aliases. Müller was the alias he assumed in Bodæ. Some suspect Muller was, in actuality, Louis Philippe

Louis Philippe by Albert Rosenthal. *Courtesy of the Library of Congress.*

because the latter did, in fact, use Müller as an alias, and was known to have been exiled in America.

Interestingly, John E. Rodman of Philadelphia thought to ask Louis Philippe if he used his own name in America, and Louis Philippe penned a letter, which was dated August 26, 1837, explaining that he did not travel under an alias in America.

The theory that Muller was a member of French royalty in disguise seems quite preposterous today. However, in the rural village of Georgetown in the 1800s, far from the happenings of French society, rumors could run wild, with little factual basis. As aforementioned, Muller was estimated to be around fifty years old, with dark hair, a swarthy completion and black eyes. Charles X and his son, Charles Ferdinand, the Duke of Berry, were portrayed in paintings as having blond hair and fair skin. The Duke of Berry had blue eyes, and his father had brown eyes. Muller was described as close to the age of fifty when he arrived in Georgetown, somewhere between 1808 or 1809. Charles X was born in October 1757 and would have been fifty in 1807, so were it not for his fair appearance, he could have been Muller as rumored. However, it is documented that Charles X lived at 72 South Audley Street in London while in exile between 1805 and 1814. Charles Ferdinand was born in January 1778 and would have been fifty in 1828, so he was much too young to be Muller. He was also known to be living in England throughout the time Muller resided in Georgetown.

Louis Philippe did have black hair, but he was also fair-skinned. He was born in October 1773 and would have been fifty around 1823, making him also too young to be Muller. It seems rather absurd to believe that Louis Philippe could have been the mysterious Louis Muller. For one thing, Louis Philippe had no money. He, his two brothers, their servant Beaudoin, a horse and their pet dog were eking by on $1,218.50 of borrowed money that had to cover a journey across much of the eastern portion of America. They wore buckskins and did not travel in style. In fact, back when Louis Philippe had been in exile in Europe and on the run, he had actually been mistaken for a vagrant, so downtrodden was his appearance. In Philadelphia, Louis Philippe was actually denied the hand of the woman he hoped to marry in large part because of his destitute state. This hardly sounds like Louis Muller, who was said to have had hordes of gold and silver. Muller's funds were said to be an astonishing $150,000. Louis Philippe could barely afford a room. Furthermore, after his mother had been exiled to Spain, the brothers decided to return, arriving in England in 1800. They stayed there for fifteen years. Louis Muller, on the other hand, purchased his property in 1808 and lived there until around 1813, during the time Louis Philippe was known to be living in England. Louis Philippe did keep a diary of his journey around America, which his brother Montpensier skillfully illustrated with watercolors, so much of the journey of the three brothers is known. (The journal only surfaced in 1955, so this information was unavailable to the nineteenth-century residents of the Georgetown area.) Unfortunately, the second book of the journal is still unaccounted for, and the first journal ends soon after the three enter New York, leaving some of their journey open to speculation. In addition to all this, Louis Philippe, the Duke of Orleans, used his own name while traveling in America. He called himself Mr. Orleans. He had no reason to hide, for he was in America as part of a deal to free his brothers and their dog from imprisonment. His exile to America was a compromise that kept him out of the way and far from Europe. Despite the fact that he traveled in fear and under an alias in Europe, moving every two days, he felt no need to disguise his identity or hide his person in America.

When Muller left the country for the final time, he sold his property to Mr. Abijah Weston in April 1816 for $10,500. The building continued to be occupied for many years but was not maintained as it had been in Muller's time. In 1905, the Muller Mansion burned down, perhaps from a chimney fire. The building contained six fireplaces and three chimneys, but chimneys need periodic maintenance, and after Muller's exit, property maintenance was not a priority. Perhaps the chimney needed cleaning or repointing. Whatever the case, the fire was devastating, and the cherry timber mansion burned down. Now, only several pits that once were basements can be seen.

The building used to lay in what is now a state park, and the Georgetown Historical Society occasionally visits there. In fact, Jerry Dale from the Georgetown Historical Society gives a yearly tour of what remains of the property. One day, out of historical interest, Jerry Dale measured the basement of the Muller Mansion and was surprised to find it noticeably smaller than what was historically reported to be the size of the mansion. In 1893, Robert J. Hubbard (a descendant of Thomas H. Hubbard, Muller's lawyer) had also visited the property while the building was still standing and reported the following in a paper to the Oneida Historical Society.

> *We descended into the cellar, and were astonished at the smallness of it. The space occupied is only about two-thirds of the size of the kitchen above. It is lighted by one small window, the sill of which, from the inner cellar wall of stone, to the outer one of the buildings is some seven feet. There is apparently no reason for this, and evidently between these two walls, is a space, some six by twenty feet with no present access to it. The owner has never gone so far as to wonder why this space exists.*

Hubbard goes on to suggest that this was a stronghold where Muller may have kept his immense wealth of gold and silver. I personally believe Muller packed his hoard and took it with him when he returned with his wife and daughters to Europe for the very last time.

According to the Georgetown Historical Society, it would be difficult organizing an archeological exploration because the Muller Mansion (or the mansion's ruins, rather) is not classified as a historic site; it is simply part of Muller Hill State Forest, a 3,090-acre forest in the town of Georgetown. The society regrets that the site has not yet achieved the protection and status of a historic site, although the forest bears Muller's name to this day.

Still, an archeological dig and site markings might benefit the site. Stories abound about the mysterious Muller. One historical reference claims that Muller would, at times, become carried away in the process of disciplining his servants, and in some instances, flogged them to death. During his 1871 visit to the Muller Mansion, Hubbard met an old woman who told him that Muller had flogged a servant to death and had the body tossed down the well outside the kitchen. When asked how she came to know this, she replied that her husband had been a servant there and had been made to fill the well after the body had been disposed down it. If this is the case, even after decades of pickers have taken bits of history from the property, a proper archeological exploration may yet find some interesting clues as to how Muller and his servants lived (and died). It may well be worthwhile.

The same old woman, in an interview with Hubbard, said "I was young... when the Frenchman lived here. They called him Mr. Muller. Some called him Phillips and said he was a king or would be in his own country. But I don't believe he was no king."

A TIBETAN MONASTERY IN CENTRAL NEW YORK

For those who long to visit a Tibetan Monastery, the trip may not be as long and arduous as expected. A quick drive to Ithaca, New York, might suffice. There you will find the Namgyal Monastery, otherwise known as the North American Seat of the Fourteenth Dalai Lama of Tibet, the earthly manifestation of Avalokiteshvara, the Buddha of Compassion.

The monastery is quite modest and is located in a building called Aurora House, an old Victorian home located on Aurora Street in downtown Ithaca. It is a simple building, with maroon siding and a yellow-gold trim. The *zafus*, or meditation cushions, inside are the same colors as the building's exterior, as are the monks' robes. Here, it is possible to meet the Dalai Lama, although one would have to wait until he is in residence and make the proper arrangements.

The Namgyal Monastery has been operating out of Aurora House since 1992, but a larger, more traditional looking monastic teaching site is in the

Namgyal Monastery door in Ithaca, New York. Namgyal Monastery is the North American seat of the Dalai Lama. *Photo courtesy of the author.*

Above: Prayer flags fly in a garden next to the Namgyal Monastery. *Photo courtesy of the author.*

Left: Outside the Namgyal Monastery in Ithaca, NY. *Photo courtesy of the author.*

works. Construction commenced several years ago, and the new monastery will be located on Tibet Drive. The progress has not been rapid, as the monastery has been under construction for almost six years at the printing of this book.

The monks at the Namgyal Monastery are known for their sand mandalas, traditional Tantric paintings formed using colored sand. They are intended to be temporary. The mandalas are blessed, and when they are dissolved away (the monks destroy the image by sweeping them away, symbolizing the impermanence of the material world), the sand from the mandalas carries the blessings in many directions into the environment. The form of the new monastery follows a central pattern of the Kalachakra sand mandala. The word Kalachakra means "time wheel" in Sanskrit.

Besides the Dalai Lama's monastery in India and Tibet, the Namgyal Monastery in Ithaca is the only one of its kind. The Dalai Lama has expressed fears that if the religious oppression in Tibet continues for another decade or more, Tibetan Buddhism may vanish in Tibet. For this reason, he established a monastery in the free world, in Ithaca, New York, as a means to

A beautiful Tibetan-style gateway indicates the entrance to Dü Khor Choe Ling, or "The Land of Kalachakra Study and Practice" in Ithaca, New York. *Photo courtesy of the author.*

Above: Detail from the gateway at Dü Khor Choe Ling. *Photo courtesy of the author.*

Left: Detail from the gateway column. *Photo courtesy of the author.*

Prayer flags can be seen from the gateway on the path to the Dü Khor Choe Ling, or "The Land of Kalachakra Study and Practice." *Photo courtesy of the author.*

preserve that venerable religion. The new monastery complex is called Dü Khor Choe Ling, or "The Land of Kalachakra Study and Practice," and it will be used for teaching, housing, dining and retreats. Though teaching is integral to the existing monastery, there is little room for students and none for student housing. Dü Khor Choe Ling began with a 2004 donation. The monastery purchased twenty-eight acres of nearby woodland to begin construction. The existing monastery on Aurora Street also houses the only Dalai Lama residence outside of India (though admittedly, the Dalai Lama is seldom in residence as he is regularly traveling the world, teaching Buddhist beliefs and educating the world on the plight of Tibet).

The story of the Ithaca monastery began in 1974, when Sidney Piburn was hiking in India. He was not altogether familiar with the Dalai Lama but did notice that he was revered and honored by the people. Curious about who this man might be, he repeatedly requested to have an audience with His Holiness. At last, his request was granted.

Piburn was unsure how the Dalai Lama would react to his visit but was quickly impressed by his unassuming nature and a quality he describes as "being so present." Piburn began showing him photos of Ithaca and asked the Dalai Lama if he would like to come there. "I have friends there, and you could stay with them," he told His Holiness. Surprisingly, the Dalai Lama agreed. Piburn was unaware that the U.S. government had just granted the Dalai Lama permission to travel in the United States.

The story of the Dalai Lama, himself, is extraordinary. The Fourteenth Dalai Lama was born on July 6, 1935, and named Lhamo Thondup, which means "Wish-Fulfilling Goddess." He lived in a tiny village that was quite poor and where the land was difficult to cultivate. His family grew barley, buckwheat and potatoes. Mostly, Lhamo Thondup acted like any other young child, but he did have two unusual habits. One was to pack a small bag and announce, "I'm going to Lhasa, I'm going to Lhasa." The other was to insist that he, three years old at the time, sit at the head of the table.

The Thirteenth Dalai Lama had died in 1933, and his body had been embalmed. However, it was customary for the body of the Dalai Lama to lie in state, and one day it was observed that the late Dalai Lama's head had turned toward the northeast. Next, the Regent had a vision, in which he saw three Tibetan letters floating in the clouds: "Ah," "Ka" and "Ma." Then he saw a monastery on a hill with a golden and turquoise roof. Finally, he saw a small home. Believing the letter "Ah" stood for the province of Amdo, a search party was dispatched to find the reincarnation of the Dalai Lama. They came to believe that "Ka" must mean the monastery at Kumbum, which resembled the one revealed to the Regent in his vision. Having this much of an indication as to where the home might be located, they began to search the surroundings of the monastery for the home that the Regent saw in his vision.

The search party visited the home but did not explain its purpose; rather, the leader feigned to be a servant so that no one would think anything of him playing with the young child. Still, the child recognized this stranger and cried, "Sera lama, Sera lama!" Indeed, he truly was a lama from the monastery of Sera. The party returned to the house after only a few days, bringing with them objects that belonged to the Thirteenth Dalai Lama and some items that were never his. The three-year-old boy recognized what had been his, crying, "Its mine. Its mine." He did not claim the other objects. The members of the search party believed they had found the true reincarnation of their old master, and he was brought back to his monastery at Lhasa to resume his life as the Fourteenth Dalai Lama.

The Dalai Lama has spent much of his life in exile and continues to champion nonviolent methods to resist Chinese religious oppression today.

CHAPTER FIVE
FINAL COMMENTS

Now that our journey into legendary Central New York has ended, I am sure some readers will remain skeptics. There are those who will say, "Fairies! Giants! Monsters! Spirits? What rubbish! It's all a bunch of humbug. Everyone knows these things are in your head. They are the product of an active imagination." Perhaps, but to that I must remind you that much of life is in your head. If a monster or the Little People are the product of our imagination with no physical basis in the natural world, then so too are the minutes and hours on a clock and the days of the week. A day is a natural concept, as is a year. An hour, a minute and the days of the week are not natural concepts but products of our human imagination. I am not suggesting that these are not useful concepts but simply that there is no natural basis for those divisions and distinctions. Surely, nature did not create Mondays. And while many of our concepts, such as our concept of hours, are not natural, both clock hours and the days of the week have a solid place in this world and always will.

Interestingly, the concepts of fairies, giants, monsters, spirits and the like that many insist do not exist can be found among completely unconnected cultures and among religiously dissimilar peoples. The concept of clock time, conversely, has been introduced to most places (rather than emerging independently) and has not existed as long. Why, then, can legendary beings be found worldwide if they do not, in fact, exist? It is a question that no one can adequately answer, but an intriguing one to ponder.

My primary purpose in writing this book and in presenting these myths, legends and curiosities is to preserve and perpetuate them. I also hope these tales make you smile, think and perhaps even cause you to recognize the rich folklore tradition that exists right in your own backyard. These are our stories after all, yet many of us are unfamiliar with the great legendary heritage that is ours here in Central New York.

When I first began writing about the folktales, legends and myths of the Central New York region, I knew there was a wealth of material to be told, but I could never have realized at that time the sheer depth and volume of the tales that have emerged. As I have watched the material unfold, I have noted, with great pleasure, that though so many elements of local folk tales correspond to lore in other parts of the world, they are also unique to this place. Central New York has historically been a place associated with mysterious happenings and beings, and the more we seek these stories, the more we discover. I sincerely hope that the reader finds this book opens new doors to that mysterious world.

All good things must end, and so must our mysterious journey through these legendary tales. But take heart, for you can always return to visit that magical world. You don't need to travel to a distant part of the globe or make complicated arrangements. You can find it all here, at home in Central New York.

BIBLIOGRAPHY

Andrlik, Todd. "The Distinction of 18th Century American Paper." "Rag Linen Online Museum of Historic Newspapers." (blog). May 1, 2010. http://raglinen.com/2010/05/01/the-distinction-of-18th-century-american-paper.

Banner of Light (Boston). "Brown's Free Hall—Inspiration and Will." January 18, 1879.

Bartholomew, Robert E., and Brian Regal. "From Wild Man to Monster: The Historical Evolution of Bigfoot in New York State." *Voices* (September 22, 2009).

Beauchamp, W. M. "Iroquois Notes." *Journal of American Folklore* 5, no 18 (1892): 223–24.

Blanchard, David. "Who or What's a Witch? Iroquois Persons of Power." *American Indian Quarterly* 6, nos. 3–4 (1982): 218–37.

Borio, Gene. "The Tobacco Timeline." Tobacco.org. Accessed March 11, 2012. http://www.tobacco.org.

Cazenovia Republican. "The Mummy Tea." February 1895.

Cazenovia Republican (Syracuse). "Odd House at Georgetown Is Monument of Devotion of Farmer to Spiritualism." November 18, 1933.

Coleman, Loren "Cryptomundo for Bigfoot, Lake Monsters, Sea Serpents and More." *Cryptomundo.* Accessed October 21, 2011. http://www.cryptomundo.com/cryptozoo-news/owasco-monster.

Converse, Harriet Maxwell, and Arthur Parker. *Myths and Legends of the New York Iroquois.* Albany, NY: privately printed, 1908. Reprint, Albany: University of the State of New York, 1981.

"Cryptomundo for Bigfoot, Lake Monsters, Sea Serpents and More." *Cryptomundo.* Accessed July 1, 2012. http://www.cryptomundo.com/cryptozoo-news/owasco-monster.

"Cryptozoo-oscity." *The Cayuga Lake Monster Aka Old Greeny.* September 17, 2009. http://cryptozoo-oscity.blogspot.com/2009/09/cayuga-lake-monster-aka-old-greeny.html.

Dann, Norman K. *Practical Dreamer: Gerrit Smith and the Crusade for Social Reform.* Hamilton, NY: Log Cabin, 2009.

Davis, Margaret P. *Honey out of the Rafters: A Pictorial History of the Settlement and Growth of Steuben and Remsen, NY.* Boonville, New York: Boonville Graphics, 1976.

Dennis, Matthew. "American Indians, Witchcraft, and Witch-hunting." *OAH Magazine of History* 17.4 (2003): 21-27.

Ford, Ann. Letter to Edith and Richard Monsour. September 25, 1991. Personal collection of Edith and Richard Monsour. Vernon, NY.

"From Birth To Exile." *The Official Website for The Office of His Holiness the 14th Dalai Lama.* Accessed May 14, 2012. http://www.dalailama.com/biography/from-birth-to-exile.

"The Gifts of the Little People." *Kahonwes's Mohawk & Iroquois Index.* Accessed March 27, 2012. http://www.kahonwes.com/iroquois/littlepe.htm.

Godwin, Joscelyn. *The Spirit House, or Brown's Free Hall in Georgetown, NY: A Short History.* Hamilton, NY: The Upstate Institute at Colgate University, 2011.

Goodman, Jordan. *Tobacco in History: The Cultures of Dependence*. London: Routledge, 1994.

Herrick, James W., and Dean R. Snow. *Iroquois Medical Botany*. Syracuse, NY: Syracuse University Press, 1995.

Hubbard, Robert J. Diary of Robert James Hubbard's world tour, 1893. Lorenzo State Historic Society Site, Cazenovia, NY.

———. *"The Mystery of the Muller Mansion."* Transcript of reading at the Oneida Historical Society, Oneida, NY 1893.

Huron Expositor. "Two Dreams and What Became of Them." December 12, 1890.

"Into the Land of Kalachakra." *Connecting Great Media Projects and the Funding Community*. Accessed April 5, 2012. http://media.gfem.org/node/10866.

Johnson, Elias. *Legends, Traditions and Laws, of the Iroquois, or Six Nations: And History of the Tuscarora Indians*. Lockport, NY: Union Printing, 1881.

K., E.E. "John Brown in Vernon." n.d.

Leveille, Madeleine, and John R. McKivigan. "The 'Black Dream' of Gerrit Smith, New York Abolitionist." *The Courier* 20, no. 2 (1985): 51–76. http://surface.syr.edu/libassoc/176/.

Logan, Adelphena. *Memories of Sweet Grass*. Washington Depot, CT: Shiver Mountain Press 1979.

"Madison County, New York." Rootsweb. Last modified May 14, 2011. http://www.rootsweb.ancestry.com/%7Enymadiso.

Morgan, Lewis Henry. *League of the Iroquois*. 2nd edition. Seacaucus, New Jersey: Carol Publishing Group, 1993.

New York Christian Inquirer. "Obituary of J. Whipple Jenkins Esq." November 6, 1852.

"Owasco Lake Monster." *Syracuse.com History Records*. Accessed January 13, 2012. http://blog.syracuse.com/strangecny/2007/12/history_records_owasco.

Parker, Arthur C. "Part 2: Field Notes On The Rites And Ceremonies Of The Ganio`Dai'io` Religion." In *Iroquois Maize and Other Food Plants, The Code of Handsome Lake the Seneca Prophet, The Constitution of the Five Nations*. 1913. Reprint, Syracuse, NY: Syracuse University Press, 1968.

Porterfield, Amanda. "Witchcraft and the Colonization of Algonquian and Iroquois Cultures." *Religion and American Culture* 2.1 (1992): 103–24.

Rice, Carlton. "Spiritual Temple." *The DeRuyter Gleaner*, March 19 1896.

Robb, Edna Roberts. *Honey out of the Rock: Mel O'r Craig*. Arlington, VA: Self-published, 1960.

Smith, E.A. *Myths of the Iroquois*. Cambridge: Harvard University, 1883.

Southworth, G. "Builders of Our Country I." Heritage History. Accessed March 2012. http://www.heritage history.com/www/heritagebooks.php?Dir'books&MenuItem'display&author'southworth&book'builders1&story'johnson.

Utica Daily Press. "Obituary of Mrs. Electra Jenkins of Vernon Died In Her Hundredth Year." 1912.

"Vernon's War Horses." n.d. Article from the private collection of Edith Monsour, Vernon, New York.

"Welcome to Namgyal." *Namgyal Monastery Institute of Buddhist Studies*. Accessed July 1, 2012. http://www.namgyal.org.

"Wild Tobacco Seed–Nicotiana Rustica from Victory Seeds." *Victory Seeds*. Accessed March 13, 2012. http://www.victoryseeds.com/nicotiana_rustica.html.

Wilson, Edmund. *Apologies to the Iroquois: With a Study of the Mohawks in High Steel*. London: W.H. Allen, 1960.

Visit us at
www.historypress.net

ABOUT THE AUTHOR

Melanie Winn Zimmer writes about New York State and performs as a storyteller and puppeteer in the Northeast and around the country. She has authored three books on New York State, including *Central New York & the Finger Lakes: Myths, Legends & Lore Lakes* and *Forgotten Tales of New York*, and has written for various publications. She is a member of the League for the Advancement of New England Storytelling and the New York Folklore Society. You may visit her website at www.thepuppets.com.

Melanie Zimmer. *Photograph courtesy of Francis Zimmer.*